Bucks County Adventures

From William Penn
and George Washington to Neil Armstrong

By
Carl LaVO

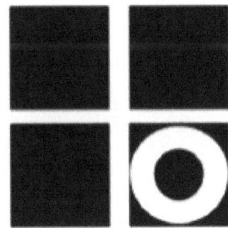

Open Door Publications

Bucks County Adventures
From William Penn and George Washington to Neil Armstrong

ISBN: 978-0-9981208-0-5

Cover Design by Genevieve LaVO Cosdon, LaVODesign.com

Published by
Open Door Publications
2113 Stackhouse Dr.
Yardley, PA 19067
www.OpenDoorPublications.com

Dedication

To my daughter Genevieve, and my grandchildren Dashiell and Margaux, in memory of our adventures together.

The author and his wife, Mary Anne, in a photo taken in the 1970s, sitting on the tracks of the New Hope and Ivyland Railroad in Buckingham Township, Pennsylvania.

Table of Contents

New Hope's town clock,
at the Visitors Center
on Main Street.

Foreword

By Rachel Riley

As a reporter, if you asked longtime and beloved editor Carl LaVO if he had time to talk about a story, the real question was, did you have time for his answer?

More importantly, were you willing to hear it?

While he was always patient, encouraging and more than happy to listen, Carl was also filled with a plethora of endless brainstorming sessions…and he was a huge fan of a good debate.

To him, writing a story was like an archeological dig. I often teased that an example of a Carl LaVO edit would be to find any school district budget line item with the number seven in it.

But my mentor was going above and beyond doing his job. He was trying to teach me a challenging lesson: how to truly treasure hunt for that nugget that leads to a gem of a great story. To be perfectly honest, I usually walked away from his desk feeling inspired.

That's because the topic of conversation may have started with news, but it somehow usually ended up about life. For Carl, the essence of any story was the human element. Events happened, yes, but more importantly, they affected people.

In the author's *Bucks County Adventures: From William Penn and George Washington to Neil Armstrong,* Carl takes you on a journey with his family to get to know the history behind some of those events and how they affected the people of the county.

A Bucks County newsman for years, Carl lived and breathed his subject matter so his master storytelling flows like a truly great historian's should, as if he were there himself.

The author shares a Bucks County history that's even richer than one could imagine, revealing details about the likes of Henry Chapman Mercer, James A. Michener and Oscar Hammerstein.

He finds more interesting depth and tragic backstory about places you may not even know existed, including an old village or Bowman's Tower, and the simplest, most unassuming of things like Route 13 and a local community church.

With an uncanny ability to find humor in any situation, Carl will make you laugh about seemingly silly reasons why folks could've gotten arrested back in the day.

On these adventures with his daughter and grandchildren, the author discovers things about himself that he never knew. A grandfather teaching his grandson, their combined endearing innocent yet simultaneous wise view on the world, will make you smile. He'll also warm your heart, sharing personal details like where he met and fell in love with his wife, a love that continues to be celebrated today.

Carl never assumes and always wants to know more. In case you're curious, he even provides resources to help you keep the story going and maybe even find out something about yourself.

Sometimes the tale isn't about finding the right answer, or any resolution at all. It's about the process, asking the right questions. "Life's an adventure," Carl once told me. It's about the journey, who embarks on it with you and the fun you have along the way.

Rachel Riley is a former newspaper/multimedia journalist for Calkins Media from 2004 to 2014, and reported directly to Carl LaVO from 2005 to 2011.

Winter fun at Bolton Mansion in Levittown. The home, which was built in the 1600s, once was owned by William Penn's estate manager.

Introduction

Why write about Bucks County history? Hasn't everything been written that is worth writing about? Hardly.

That's the lesson I learned after being challenged a few years ago by Patricia Walker to write a weekly newspaper column centered on the county's 334-year-old history. I was a little skeptical. But Pat persisted as executive editor of the county's two daily and Sunday newspapers, the *Bucks County Courier Times* and *The Intelligencer*. After all, she stressed, I had written four books about Naval history for the Naval Institute Press in Annapolis. Certainly, as a *Courier Times* managing editor and resident of Bucks for more than 40 years, I could find some interesting things to write about locally.

I told her I'd give it a try but promised no great revelations. I began by skimming *Place Names in Bucks County Pennsylvania* by George MacReynolds. I discovered the circa-1942 book in the *Courier Times* library in Levittown. Inside were brief but tantalizing tales I knew nothing about. To follow up on them, I invited my daughter, son-in-law and grandchildren to make an adventure of visiting places the book described. We'd then figure out how these places evolved in county history, enlarging on stories rooted to 50, 100, 200, 300 years ago. Before long, we had explored back roads to historic sites, checked ancient archives like Doylestown's Spruance Library of the Bucks County Historical Society and talked to people from one end of the county to the other. Our journey has taken us hiking up the slopes of Haycock Mountain to stand atop massive volcanic boulders. We've stepped into a boat that carried George Washington and his army across the Delaware River. We've followed woodland trails to the ruins of a fabled estate in Lower Bucks, and kayaked among beaver dams to understand the history of an exotic pond in Tinicum Township. We've visited the home of a Broadway legend, a mountaintop church that once sheltered runaway slaves from the South and the centrifuge where the first man who landed on the moon once trained for his mission.

The response from readers to our adventures has been overwhelming, many suggesting this book. "Your column," said reader Mandy Capella, "reminds me of how truly blessed I am to live in such a wonderful area as Bucks County." She and others continue to inspire us and provide new mysteries to resolve, and unusual sites to visit. The list of ideas is long and getting longer. The family fun continues.

I hope you enjoy these selected works and gather the sense of history and beauty that makes Bucks County extraordinary. My hope is this book adds to your own enjoyment of a very special place.

Carl LaVO
November, 2016

THE DURHAM BOATS

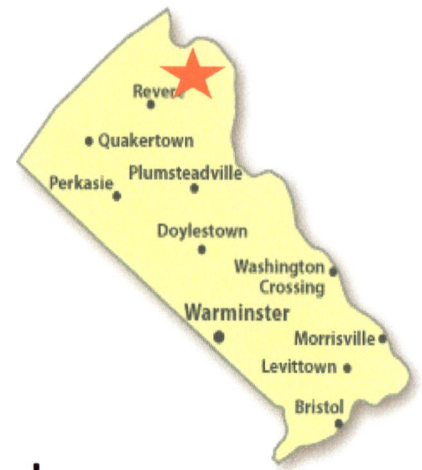

The Boats That Ensured

Washington's Crossing of the Delaware

Welcoming sign in Durham Township .

THE CHALLENGE WAS SIMPLE: "Let's go find an oven where cannon balls were made and boats built to carry George Washington and thousands of soldiers across the Delaware River on Christmas."

Genevieve, Dashiell and Margaux were eager, to say the least. So we piled in the car and headed to the postcard village of Durham in Upper Bucks to begin our adventure. The town easily can be missed since it sits down the slope of Mine Hill just off State Highway 213. The settlement of about two dozen Victorian homes and an ancient grist mill sits on a tributary to the nearby Delaware. At first we zoomed past the village, then doubled back to a small roadside marker pointing the way down the hill. From a website, I knew the Durham Blast Furnace was located near the town post office. But we couldn't see anything resembling the forge built in 1727. To our surprise, how-

Famous painting of Washington crossing the Delaware by Emanuel Luetze.

ever, we spied a Durham boat under an open-air pavilion in a pocket park. Wooden steps led to the vessel's topside, inviting visitors to explore the 40-foot-long craft. Cool! In a snap, all four of us scampered aboard. Dash took charge of a 16-foot-long tiller at the stern as if steering through a make-believe current. We walked planks running the length of the deck where boatmen once shouldered iron-tipped poles to push the boat through river shallows. We climbed down to the keel, peered into a dark hold and studied oar locks and paddles.

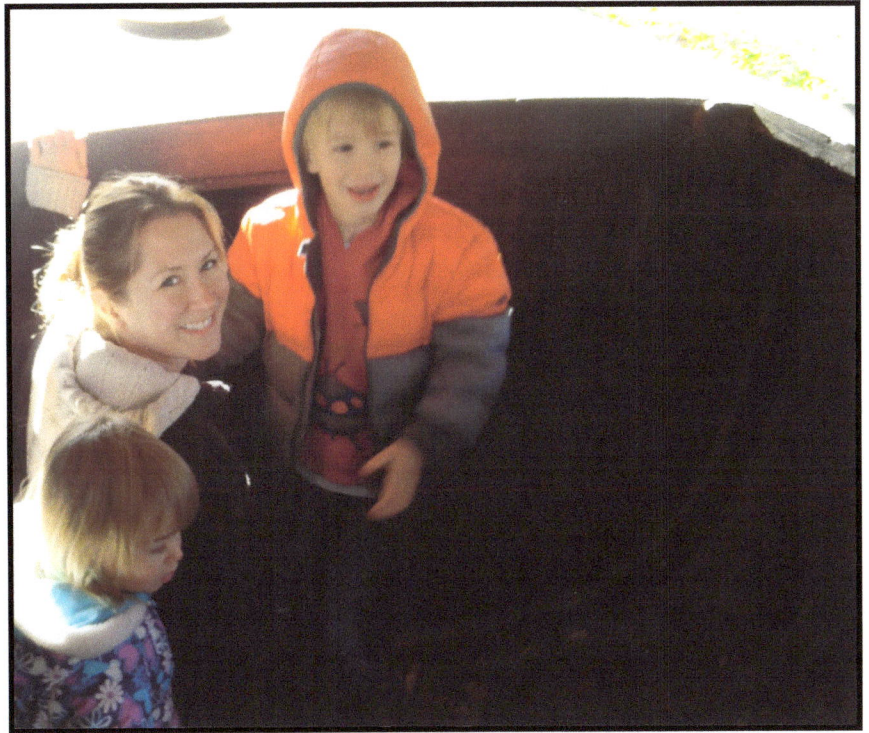

Margaux, Genevieve and Dashiell in the hold at the stern of the Durham boat.

The boat's design was conceived by Robert Durham in 1730. The vessels were needed to carry pig iron from the new blast furnace down the Delaware to markets in Bristol and Philadelphia. Durham's boat was similar to skiffs used by early Scandinavian settlers. At 66 feet long and pointed at both ends, it was flat-bottomed, 6 feet wide and 3 feet deep. When fully loaded with 17 tons of cargo, it could float in water only 20 inches deep—perfect for navigating river shoals. Crewmen used oars when the river was deep enough. Durham's boats became ubiquitous. A fleet of 1,000 with 6-man crews dominated river commerce. There were so many by 1776 when George Washington contemplated crossing the Delaware that he commandeered dozens to move his army. Others delivered rifle and cannon shot from the Durham furnace.

Grandson Dashiell takes the tiller of the boat in Durham Township in Upper Bucks alongside sister, Margaux, and the author.

Our objective in Durham was to find that forge. About to give up, we saw a middle-aged couple raking leaves in front of their home. "The furnace is in the hillside near the parking lot, right in front of the grist mill," we were told. "It's very small." Indeed. Backtracking we found it, looking much like a brick-lined Hobbit hole. It was about 4 feet high and 8 feet deep. Wow! Hard to believe such a small furnace could manufacture all the ammo for Washington's guns as well as iron for "Adam and Eve" wood-burning stoves sold all over the Delaware River Valley in the 1700s. Later we found out what we had been inspecting was a Revolutionary War oven used to produce coal for the furnace that used to exist, now replaced by the grist mill.

"Well, kids," I implored. "Let's go see how far it is to Washington Crossing where the boats were used to get Washington across the Delaware." It took more than an hour on a 60-mile stretch of winding River Road. Enough daylight remained for

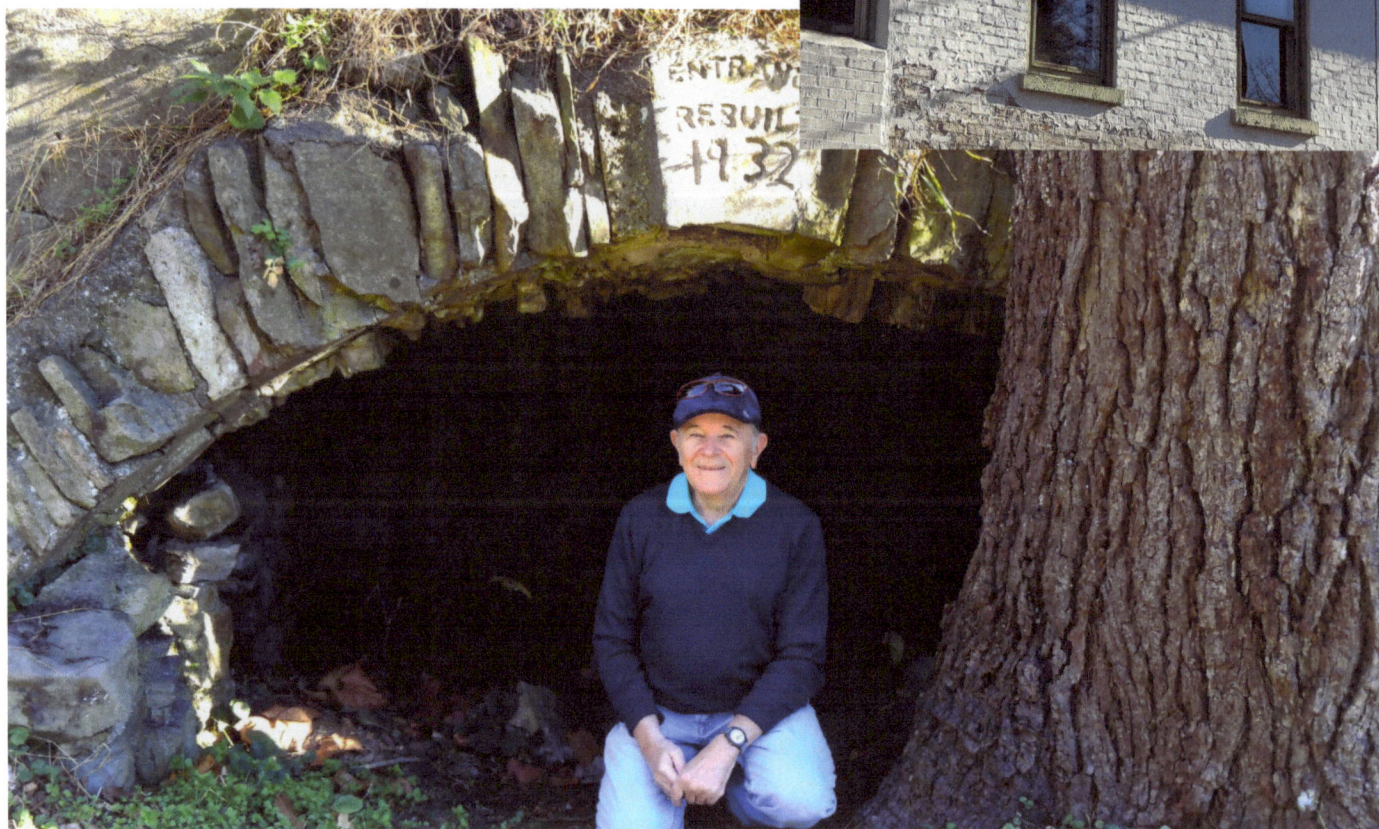

Above right, an ancient grist mill now covers what once was a blast furnace that produced munitions that were shipped on Durham River boats to George Washington's army during the American Revolution. Bottom center, the author kneeling in front of what turned out to be a stone oven used to produce coal for the Durham blast furnace.

Another view of the grist mill, which covers the remains of the Revolutionary War era blast furnace.

us to visit the park's museum and collection of four Durham boats stacked in a barn to protect them. They were about to be moved to the river where people dressed as soldiers and officers including one playing George Washington would oar across the Delaware on Christmas Day to re-enact the famous crossing prior to the Battle of Trenton 240 years ago. That in its way, I told my grandchildren, led to the creation of the United States.

Dash saw a print of "Washington Crossing the Delaware" propped on an easel near the boats. "Look, Margaux, there's George Washington!"

More information can be found in "History of the Durham Boat" by the Durham Historical Society.

Margaux standing on the keel of a Durham boat, the type that carried George Washington and the Continental Army across the Delaware River on Christmas 1776 to win his first big battle in Trenton, N.J.

The fabulous interior of Doylestown's Mercer Museum, which
displays a vast collection of Early American life on seven
floors and an open atrium.

Design of Bucks' Famed Covered Bridges Led to an Unknown Family Connection

Window at mid-span of the Schofield Ford Covered Bridge in Newtown Township.

THE SCHOFIELD FORD COVERED BRIDGE in Tyler State Park is a marvel to behold. At 170 feet, it's the longest of a dozen covered bridges in Bucks County that date back to the 1800s. What's visually impressive are its crossbeams forming a lattice tied together by wooden pegs. They give the bridge incredible beauty, strength and durability.

One man who mastered that technique was Henry Grow Jr. of nearby Montgomery County. Born in 1817, he was the son of a Lutheran farm family in Ardmore. As a teen, he became an apprentice carpenter who studied the architecture of wooden bridges. By age 25, he constructed and maintained covered bridges for the Philadelphia, Germantown and Norristown railroad and other clients in the region.

Though Grow was doing well in his new occupation, he had a falling out with his family over religion in 1842. Mor-

Henry Grow Jr., the author's fifth generation grandfather who designed and built covered bridges in Pennsylvania before moving west to Salt Lake City.

had a falling out with his family over religion in 1842. Mormon missionaries had converted him and his wife into the fledgling Church of Jesus Christ of Latter Day Saints by baptizing them in the Delaware River in Bucks County. Spurned by his family, the couple left the area. They journeyed west with many stops, eventually leading to the remote Mormon settlement of Salt Lake City in the wilds of Utah. Arriving in 1851, Grow went to work building the territory's first suspension bridges over four rivers using the lattice method seen today in the covered bridges of Bucks County.

Mormon leader Brigham Young was so impressed he approached Grow with a far-fetched idea: Could he use his bridge-building skills to construct a sanctuary that could seat 9,000 under an interior dome with no visible supports? After much consideration, Grow said it was feasible.

Construction got underway in 1862. Workers laid out great center arches on the ground, then positioned them atop 20-foot-high supporting stone buttresses at the edges of the edifice. The resulting archway created an interior roof 65 feet

Entrance to the 170-foot-long Schofield Ford Covered Bridge.

high over a cavernous seating area, which was much wider and nearly as long as a football

Interior of the Schofield Ford Covred Bridge shows the wooden lattice work that gives it strength and beauty—a design that carried the author's ancestral grandfather to fame in pioneer Utah in the late 1800s.

field. The finished sanctuary—the Mormon Tabernacle—opened on Oct. 6, 1867 to a capacity crowd of 12,000. Grow touted the building on his business cards as "the largest Hall in the world unsupported by columns."

The business card of Henry Grow Jr. who constructed the domed Mormon Tabernacle.

For 30 years, he continued as a church leader, architect and builder of homes, bridges and businesses in Utah. His works include the Deseret Paper Mill to supply the city newspaper.

In his lifetime, he had many offspring including a granddaughter, Millie Melville. She had a daughter Ivy who fell deeply in love with an Army horse soldier from Texas who was not a church member. Ivy gave up Mormonism to marry that soldier, Carl Flornoy LaVO. They moved to San Francisco where Ivy bore her husband a son – my father, Carl Palmer.

In my childhood, I knew little about the Mormons but learned from my 100-year-old great grandma Millie that her grandfather Henry was the architect of the famous hall where the Mormon Tabernacle Choir performed on radio and TV. That was the extent of my knowledge about him. That is, until I made my own journey here from California through Florida. When I arrived in my late 20s, I loved traveling up River Road along the Delaware and taking side trips through the covered bridges of Erwinna, Tinicum, Solebury and other towns. My interest in them eventually led to Henry Grow Jr. and family roots I never knew I had in Pennsylvania and Bucks County.

The Uhlerstown covered bridge over the Delaware Canal in Upper Bucks is one of 12 preserved in the county.

FALLING IN LOVE IN FALLSINGTON

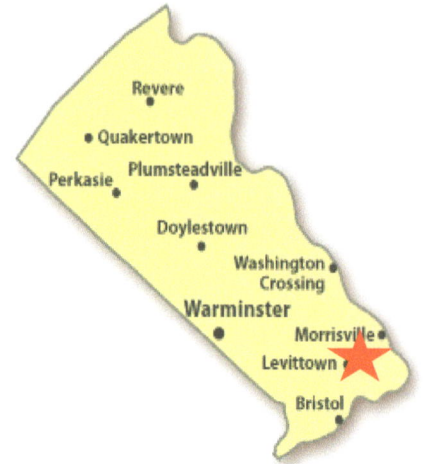

Falls Township Festival
Sparks 40-Year Tradition

Fallsington's monument to World War I's fallen soldiers from the village.

ON THE SECOND SATURDAY of every October, Mary Anne and I visit a familiar village green as we've done annually for the past 42 years. It's there we met in 1974.

As a newspaper reporter at the time, I was on assignment covering the 21st annual Historic Fallsington Day. Residents that Saturday portrayed livelihoods that existed three centuries earlier in the Falls Township hamlet. Many dressed in period garb, opened their homes to tours and told tales of olden times. In Meetinghouse Square beside the Stage Coach Tavern and across from a log house built in the 1600s, an actor dressed like Robin Hood quoted Shakespearean verse on a wooden stage while volunteers served up hot apple cider in the crisp autumn air. Children skipped around a ribbon-draped maypole on the green. Others climbed aboard horse-dawn farm wagons that rumbled past Colonial and Victorian homes and into the square where a towering sugar maple splashed red against the blue sky.

Fallsington began as a Dutch trading post at the intersection

Mary Anne and the author at their wedding in 1975 and at their daughter's wedding at the Washington Crossing Inn.

of various Indian paths. By 1683, the post became a Quaker settlement in the new colony of Pennsylvania. Sixteen years later, the village had a meetinghouse where William Penn preached for two years before returning to England.

Back then, life was tough for everyone, especially women. One wrote, "The women must prepare the deer, turkey and rabbit, to be had for the shooting, and if, as happened in one family, their one gun became disabled, the wife too went forth, and while her husband took deliberate aim, she applied the torch to the priming. Deer, besides providing meat for the skillet, supplied skins, which, tanned and dried, were stitched into trousers, shirts and moccasins. A mill was built by a large rock just west of the village and to it many of the (meetinghouse) members brought their sacks of wheat and hominy on horseback, leaving them to be ground while they went on to meeting. Some of the women came on foot from Buckingham, twenty miles away, leading their little children by the hand, carrying them over swollen streams."

Fallsington would become prosperous. By 1850, it was home to blacksmiths, a butcher, carpenters, a carriage

The Stage Coach Tavern on the central square of Fallsington where the annual celebration of Fallsington Day occurs in October.

The Burges-Lippincott home was saved from destruction in the 1950s after a developer wanted to build a gas station on the site. That led to the creation of Historic Fallsington, a preserved village of 90 buildings.

builder, farmers, an insurance agent, machinists, physicians, a surveyor and a wheelwright. A century later, farms around Fallsington became Levittown. Still, the village remained frozen in time with 90 historic buildings from the 17th, 18th, 19th and early 20th centuries. When a developer proposed a gas station near the square in 1953, citizens rallied to acquire the property. Two years later, a Falls ordinance formalized Fallsington as the state's first historic preservation district.

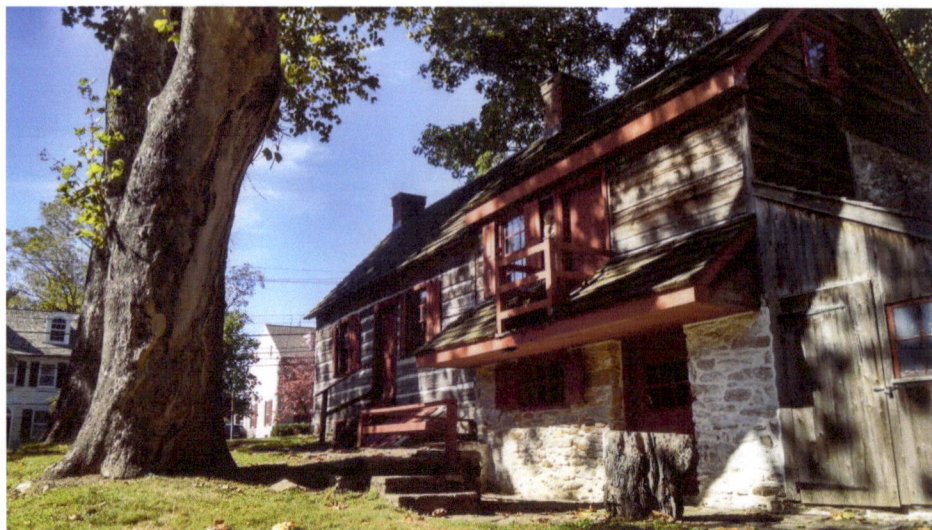

The preserved Moon-Williamson log house built in the 1760s in Historic Fallsington is one of the oldest still standing on its original site in Pennsylvania.

To Mary Anne and I, Fallsington remains a kind of firmament. It's a place we go back to time and time again to remember our beginning—the day a beautiful young woman said "hi" as I came into view. Every year on Fallsington Day, I consider the irony of that moment 42 years ago. My job as a journalist that day was to find a new angle for my story. I interviewed many visitors including a middle-aged couple from Ohio who annually returned to the village. They seemed so happy strolling the streets, hand in hand. They told me why: Fallsington Day was when they met.

How neat, I thought, not realizing that their story would become my own.

The Friends Meetinghouse in Fallsington where William Penn worshiped.

AMAZING GRACE AT MT. GILEAD

Runaway Slaves From the South Built

A Mountain Church as a Refuge Before Civil War

Above and at right, Mt. Gilead A.M.E. Church as it appears today. The historic church opens for services only a few times a year.

I'VE LONG ADMIRED Bucks County's legacy of sheltering runaway slaves before the Civil War. I first became aware of it in the 1970s when Mary Anne and I as newlyweds moved to Anna and Charlie Simons' farm in Buckingham. In the early spring, Anna invited us to join them for Easter Sunrise services in an old church atop Buckingham Mountain a mile away. Mt. Gilead was built in the 1830s and was part of a network of safe places in the state for slaves fleeing captivity in the South. At the time of our visit, the church was shuttered most of the year. But on Easter and Memorial Day, descendants would arrive from all over the region to recall the struggle for freedom and remember how area farmers guarded the mountain's wooded hideout from Southern slave catchers. I've seen tears roll down the cheeks of blacks and whites at those incredibly moving services. They inspired Mary Anne to write a newspaper story to bring Mt. Gilead to public attention. And it was Mt. Gilead's congregation that baptized our daughter, Genevieve, in the 1980s.

Given this, it's jarring to realize how Bucks County em-

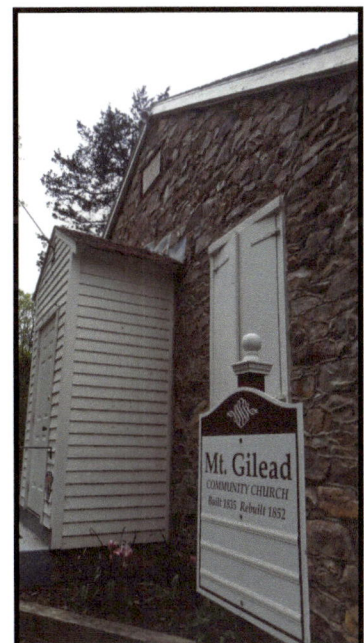

braced slavery for 185 years. Dutch immigrants brought it here in 1639. By the time of William Penn's arrival in 1681, Quakers had their own slaves. Penn joined in. In 1685, as James Harri-

William Penn purchased slaves to build his home in Tullytown.

son was building Pennsbury Manor in Falls, he anguished over difficulty retaining hired help. Replied Penn, "It were better they were blacks, for then we might have them for life." Six months later he purchased about a dozen and advised Harrison, "The blacks of Captain Allen I have as good as bought, so part not with them without my order."

Church members outside Mt. Gilead.

Penn came to abhor slavery. In 1701, he ordered freedom for his slaves at his death. Slavery lived on and spread, however. Samuel Hart recalled that in 1785 "I could stand on a corner of my father's farm (on the Old York road near Warminster), commanding an extensive view of a country beautifully situated, and naturally of excellent quality, and from

Church members and visitors gather around the grave of a Mt. Gilead founder as his descendant reads the Gettysburg Address on Memorial Day in 1980.

Harriet Tubman is memorialized in Bristol's waterfront park for her efforts helping fugitives escape slavery in the South prior to the Civil War.

that spot I could count 16 farmhouses, and in every house were slaves more or less."

About half the black slave population in Bucks lived on Dutch farms in Bensalem and the Hamptons. Another third lived in Quaker-dominated Falls, Middletown, the Makefields, the Bristols and Wrightstown. Unlike conditions in the South, local slaves lived in their owners' homes and were treated much like family. Records indicate they were well fed, well clothed and cared for when sick. However, if any strayed without a pass, they could be imprisoned. If no owners showed up, they were sold to recover costs. Often that meant shipment to the Deep South where conditions were grim and escape impossible.

In 1688, Philadelphia Quakers initiated the drive to outlaw state slavery. Abolitionists elsewhere took up the cause and established safe houses for fugitives headed to freedom in Canada—the so-called "Underground Railroad." By the late 1700s, Rep. Matthew Hughes of Buckingham became the first lawmaker in the state Assembly to move a bill that would abolish slavery in 1779. Freedom would come at a crawl ,however. A state-ordered registry of all slaves in Pennsylvania in 1782 listed 520 in Bucks out of a population of 20,119. It wasn't until 1824 that the last—two girls, 10 and 8, and a boy, 6—were set free by Doylestown's Ann Bering on condition they remain indentured servants until age 28.

Rep. Hughes lived to 100 and is buried at the Quaker Meeting in Buckingham. Occasionally, I like to make the drive to the top of Buckingham Mountain to recall the story that is told every Easter Sunday at sunrise at Mt. Gilead. I'll also think about Memorial Day in the churchside cemetery where impassioned descendants of those buried will recite the Gettysburg Address.

William Penn's home in Tullytown known as Pennsbury Manor.

A CASTLE FOR AUNT LELA

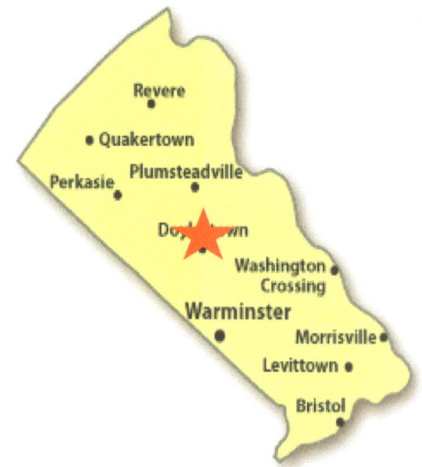

Castle in Doylestown Built

To Memorialize Beloved Aunt

Portrait of Elizabeth Chapman Lawrence, daughter of a Bucks County judge who married into the wealthy Bigelow family of Boston and became an international celebrity.

NOVELIST CHARLES DICKENS CALLED HER "that little darling." English satirist William Thackerey said she was "easy to fall in love with"—and he did. Henry Adams modeled his heroine after her in his best-seller *Democracy*. She considered American President James Buchanan "an immense friend." She thought of Sen. Henry Clay the "most distinguished" person she'd ever seen. She charmed aristocrats, artists, writers, business moguls and government leaders at home and abroad. In private she could be cutting. She danced with Prince Albert and later characterized his wife, British Queen Victoria, as "that little dumpy red-faced staring queen." She pitied poor Albert for "having to pass all his days with the singular mixture of red pepper & ice that stood by his side." At home, she compared Abraham Lincoln to "a grunt" in a pig's litter after traveling Italy with good friend Gen. George McClellan whom Lincoln relieved of command of Union forces in the Civil War. Her life was a whirl, and she would be memorialized in a castle she didn't live to see. Without her, Fonthill in Doylestown might never have been built.

So who was "Auntie Lela"?

Henry Chapman Mercer as a teenager.

Elizabeth Chapman led a life of privilege from her birth in 1829 to Bucks County Judge Henry Chapman and wife Rebecca, a dark-eyed beauty of Scotch-Irish ancestry. At age 25, Elizabeth married diplomat T. Bigelow Lawrence, a GQ-worthy attaché in London who later became American consul-general to Italy. Lawrence was scion of the enormously wealthy Lawrence family of Boston. For 15 years, the debonaire couple cut the rug in social circles in Washington, London, Italy and elsewhere in Europe, crossing paths with luminaries of the age. But at

Interior of the castle showing Henry's unique Mercer ceramic tiles.

the inauguration of Gen. Ulysses Grant as U.S. president in 1869, Lawrence contracted a severe illness and died at age 45. His multimillion dollar estate passed to his wife. Childless at age 39, she sustained her lifestyle lavishly. Her vivacious personality and friendships made her a constant subject of social commentary everywhere she went.

Periodically, she returned to Doylestown to live for months at a time with her sister, Mary Mercer. It was during those visits that she took tutorial interest in Mary's two young sons, Henry and Willie, who called her "Auntie Lela." It was Henry who became the apple of her eye. She paid for his education at Harvard and the University of Pennsylvania Law School.

Henry Chapman Mercer built Fonthill Castle in Doylestown in memory of Elizabeth Chapman, his "Auntie Lela."

She also funded his trips abroad.

Henry spent most of the 1880s in Europe and Egypt studying architecture and archeology. At home, he helped found the Bucks County Historical Society and became museum manager for what was to become the University of Pennsylvania. In his travels, he amassed a huge collection of American Industrial Age and pre-Columbia objects he thought might be lost forever. What to do with them? Enter Auntie Lela. She contributed seed money to pay for what was to become the Mercer Museum, a seven-story, 55-room concrete monolith in Doylestown where the collection was permanently exhibited. She also hired builders to construct an Italian villa known as Aldie in Doylestown for her retired father and sister Mary's family.

Above, England's Prince Albert whom "Auntie Lela" felt sorry for. Below, Charles Dickens considered Lela "that little darling."

Queen Victoria whom Lela characterized as "a red-faced staring queen."

Elizabeth, 76, died from pneumonia in 1905 before the museum opened. She left the bulk of her estate to Henry who used it to build Fonthill Castle in Doylestown. With 44 rooms, it would be Mercer's home and a memorial to the guiding hand of his beloved aunt. Colorful ceramic tiles made in Henry's kilns decorate the castle as a testament to her.

Through the years, little was known publicly about Auntie Lela. But in 1980 a Fonthill worker discovered a breadbox in the castle's off-limits tower. Inside the tin were 200 letters written by Henry's aunt during her travels. The missives were on stationery in tiny script. Some ran 10 pages, front to back. Carefully deciphered, they revealed at last the life and times of Elizabeth Chapman Lawrence.

Additional details of Elizabeth Lawrence's life can be found in E.L.: The Bread Box Papers *by Helen Hartman Gemmill.*

Nephew Henry Mercer built a bonfire on the castle roof one night to prove to skeptical Doylestown residents the building would not burn down

Bucks County Safeguarded the Man Who Killed Alexander Hamilton

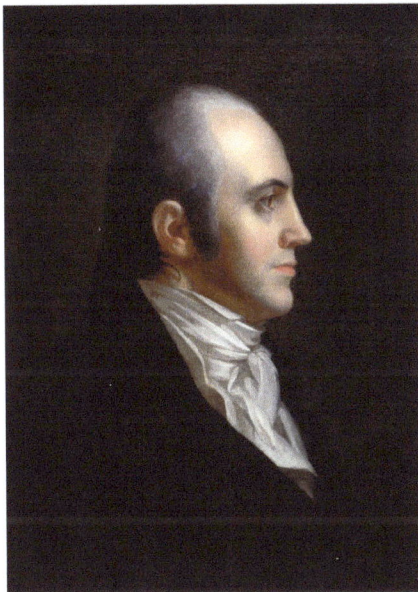

Aaron Burr in fleeing murder charges in New York fled to Bucks County by crossing over the Delaware River about a mile upstream from the King George II Inn located in Bristol.

THE HOTTEST TICKET ON BROADWAY is the hip-hop musical "Hamilton" glorifying Alexander Hamilton. In the context of the play, I think Aaron Burr got a bum deal. Branded an assassin after killing Hamilton in a pistol duel on the banks of the Hudson River, Burr fled to Bristol and then to Falls Township to escape arrest.

The Burr-Hamilton duel remains the most famous in U.S. history and was held to settle a long and bitter grudge between the former friends. Here's the LaVO Notes version of what happened:

Hamilton, like Burr, served on George Washington's staff during the Revolution. In the early days of the republic, Hamilton was the Big Dog of New York state politics and a member of the conservative Federalist Party. Tapped by Washington to be the nation's first treasury secretary, he set monetary policy, raised funds to pay off wartime debts and conceived the first central bank. Burr, who had fallen out of favor with Washington during the war, was a rising star of the liberal Democrat-Republican Party. After becoming New York attorney general, he won election in 1791 to the U.S. Senate seat held by Hamilton's father-in-law. Stunned, Hamilton and his allies campaigned relentlessly to blacken Burr's reputation behind his back.

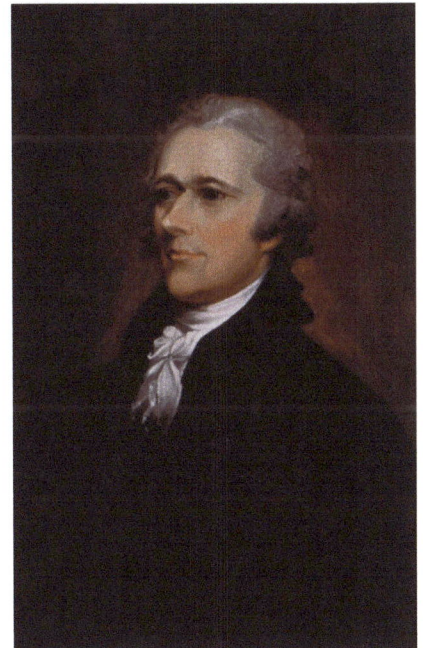

Portrait of Alexander Hamilton.

In the presidential election of 1800, Burr ran as vice president on the Democratic-Republican ticket with Thomas Jefferson as the presidential nominee. The two opposed John Adams, the Federalist incumbent president, and his vice president Charles Pinckney. The popular vote was close, requiring the Electoral College to decide the outcome. Burr and Jefferson finished on top—in a tie. It fell to the House of Representatives to break the tie.

Aaron Burr fires the fatal shot in the famous duel with Alexander Hamilton.

Hamilton seized the day. He used his influence in the Federalist-dominated chamber to get Jefferson elected president by a single vote, making Burr the VP.

The rivalry only got worse the following year when a Burr ally killed Hamilton's eldest son in a pistol duel.

Near the end of Burr's term, Hamilton described him in a New York newspaper as a "most despicable . . . dangerous man who ought not to be trusted with the reins of government." Infuriated, Burr demanded Hamilton renounce the lies. He refused. Burr challenged him to a duel, perfectly legal at the time. Hamilton agreed.

On the morning of July 11, 1804, the two men crossed the Hudson from Manhattan in row boats to settle their quarrel. Beneath brownstone cliffs at the exact place where Hamilton's son died, Hamilton fired first, barely missing. Burr returned fire. The ball fractured Hamilton's ribs and pierced his liver and diaphragm. He succumbed the next day at age 49.

Supporters sought murder changes as Burr fled. Reaching the Delaware River in Burlington, N.J., he boarded the Bloomsdale Ferry that took him to today's intersection of Green Lane and Radcliffe Street in Bristol. There he rested at the ferry hotel before being taken in by William and Elizabeth Satterthwaite at their Quaker farm in Falls. Later Burr fled to the safety of Charles Biddle in Philadelphia and then to his daughter's home in South Carolina.

When murder charges in New York and New Jersey were dropped, Burr returned to Washington to serve out the remainder of his term as vice president. By then, he regretted what had happened and delivered a farewell address to a tearful Senate. Burr later was tried for treason on dubious charges and acquitted. Afterwards, he retired to New York and died in obscurity at age 80.

The flight of Aaron Burr to Bucks County is recounted in Place Names in Bucks County *by George MacReynolds published in 1942.*

The iconic Grundy Mill on the Delaware Canal in Bristol where, in the 19th century, barges laden with coal arrived for delivery to Philadelphia.

THE RINGING ROCKS

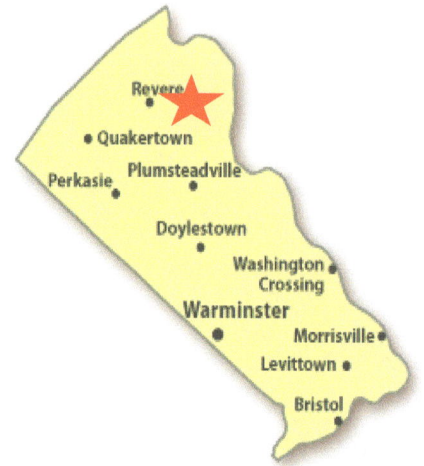

It's Official:

The Icons of Bucks County

Official flag of Bucks County .

OUR GOAL WAS TO FIND A PLACE where all the "official" symbols of Bucks County could be found. It dawned on me that Ringing Rocks in Upper Bucks might be that place. So I asked my grandchildren Dashiell and Margaux, "Hey, kids, how about an adventure at a place where you can make rocks chime like a bell?" I explained how we'd also be on the lookout for a certain flag, animal, fish, flower, bird and tree. So, with parents Michael and Genevieve, we moseyed up Lonely Cottage Road into the highlands of Bridgeton Township to Ringing Rocks County Park. We came prepared with hammers to tap the boulders and were on the lookout to see what we could see.

First item on our list: the ringing rocks, of course. The stones are made of diabase, which is the official rock of Bucks County. The grayish-brown boulders piled up on one another were produced by volcanos in prehistoric times, causing the minerals inside to line up like strings on a violin.

When struck, each produces a tone similar to a musical instrument. If cracked open, the mineral strings are broken and lose their musicality.

In 1890, Pleasant Valley physician John Ott gave a musical performance at the boulder field using a steel hammer to ring 200-pound stones of different shapes. To the accompaniment of a brass band, he played "Home Sweet Home" among the tunes. Ringing Rocks—covering 7 acres in the 128-acre park—was purchased in 1894 by a Frenchtown, N.J. banker to protect them at a time when a manufacturer of Belgian blocks wanted to quarry the

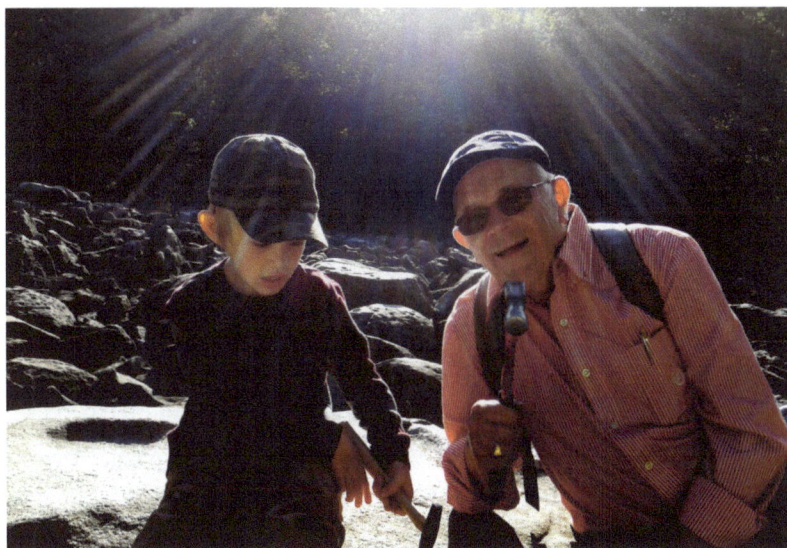

The author and his grandson ready to chime the perfect rock.

stones. Eventually, county government took possession and created the park. Ringing Rocks is only rivaled by three others in the world: the Musical Stones of Skiddaw in the English Lake District, the Ringing Rocks of Kiandra in New South Wales, Australia, and the Bell Rock Range of Western Australia.

We happily scrambled about the stones of our Ringing Rocks, using our tap hammers to create a symphony that only Mozart might appreciate.

Our next objective was easy: finding the **official bird**. That's a cardinal. Only the male is red and easy to spot. He's the Donald Trump of the bird world, fierce at protecting his territory. After driving out intruders, he'll perch on a favorite tree and chortle away in song. Cardinals are long lived, averaging 15 years.

Official Bucks County flower, the violet.

The **official tree** was easy, too. The dogwood's leaves are some of the earliest to turn color in the fall. In 16th century England, canines enjoyed resting beneath the boughs. Thus the trees were known as "dog-trees" and eventually "dogwood." In early America where dogwoods were plentiful, pioneers gathered their twigs, peeled off the bark and used them to scrub their teeth.

We skulked around the edges of Ringing Rocks to find the **official flower,** the violet. In mythology, Greek love goddess Aphrodite's sacred flower was the violet, and it became the symbol of ancient Athens. Obvi-

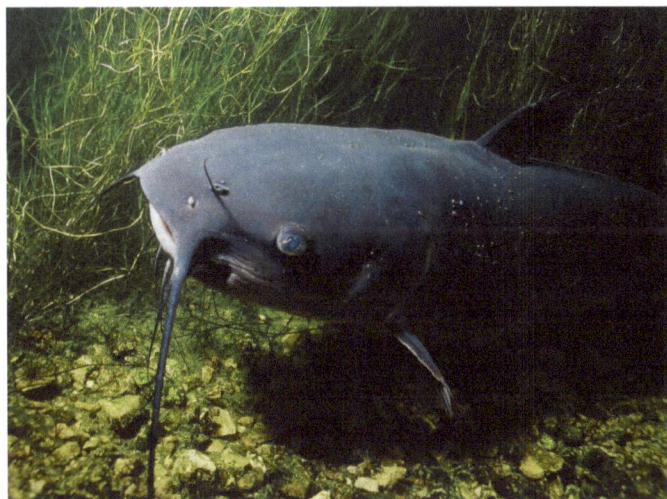

Official fish of Bucks County, the channel catfish.

ously, Aphrodite loves Bucks with its proliferation of her flower.

The **official animal** was hiding. The cottontail rabbit had plenty of hiding places among the rocks, in hollows and along the park's running stream and waterfall. At a top speed of 18 mph, the cottontail can zig and zag in a blur.

While looking for the rascally rabbit, we came across the **official seal** on a park sign and the side of a ranger's truck. It was in March 1683 that Pennsylvania founder William Penn ordered his governing council to create a seal that would show a tree and a vine. As he noted, "the woods yield us plums, grapes, peaches, strawberries and chestnuts in abundance." The council added Penn's family crest.

Official mammal, the cottontail rabbit.

Official bird, the cardinal.

For the **official fish—** the channel catfish—we had to come down off the hill about a mile to the Delaware Canal and Delaware River, which are loaded with them. The biggest ever caught in Pennsylvania weighed more than 35 pounds and was pulled from the nearby Lehigh Canal in 1991. What's interesting is the male catfish prepares the nest for his mate to lay up to 50,000 eggs. He then is left to defend the little ones.

Finding the **official flag** would complete the quest. None to be seen. I contacted county Commissioner Diane Marseglia. "Where can we find the Bucks flag flown outside?" She was stumped and got back to me: Only one place...outside the new county courthouse in Doylestown. The commissioners designed the flag in 1962. The official county seal is embroidered against a background of Bucks' official colors— blue and gold. There's a green band around the seal. It represents the county's natural beauty that continues to attract visitors.

With our adventure at an end, I revealed that school kids in Bucks chose the official rock, animal, tree, flower, bird and fish. Should the county also have an **official bug**? "Spider!" demanded Dash after seeing so many on the Ringing Rocks. Time to start a movement.

Official tree of Bucks County, the dogwood.

The Delaware Canal towpath winds through Washington Crossing Historical Park's upper section where Continental Army soldiers and an officer are buried in a memorial graveyard.

A NATURAL WONDER

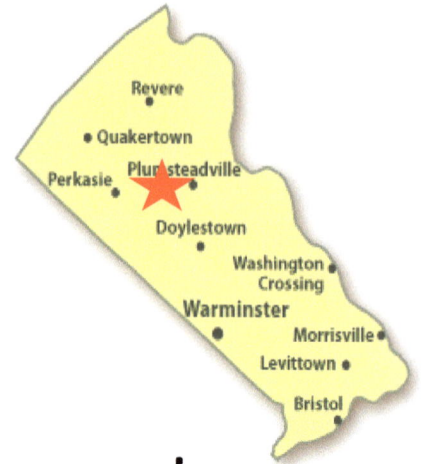

Why James Michener Gave Bucks County its Own 'Grand Canyon'

Portrait of Bucks County author James Michener who rocketed to fame with his novel *Tales of the South Pacific*.

YOU CAN'T DO BETTER THAN HEAD TO HIGH ROCKS if you own a dog. Doug Gilbert rates the cliffs among the best in his *55 Places to Hike with Your Dog in the Philadelphia Region*. He notes, "Two hundred feet below you stretches a hillside tapestry of trees collared by a horseshoe turn in the Tohickon Creek. There is no similar view in the Delaware Valley."

I agree with him, having taken in most of the sights in Bucks with a couple of four-footed companions,

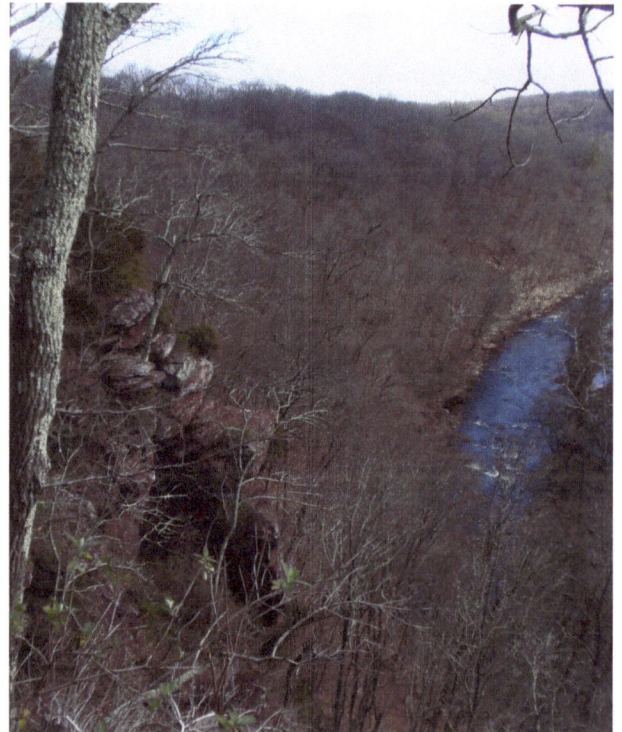

The great bend in Tohickon Creek, which carved the High Rocks that author James Michener gave to Bucks County.

Lucky and Marcel. From a parking area off Tory Road in Tinicum Township, the High Rocks trail wanders through woods to the crest of the gorge. There you can linger on a precipitous ledge or ancient cedar root. Just down the rust red cliffs are turkey vultures in their rocky lairs, taking flight within easy view and circling about in the canyon. The clear air carries the rhapsodic sound of Tohickon Creek's rapids that carved our version of the Grand Canyon. You breathe deeply and time slows down.

High Rocks was privately owned until it passed briefly in the 1940s into the hands of one of Bucks County's most famous authors. James A. Michener was none too happy about that. In a huff, he abruptly gave it away.

Michener knew about High Rocks from his childhood in the early 20th century. Young Jim loved the outdoors and belonged to the Boys Brigade of Doylestown. "We had a wonderful three weeks of real camping out and canoes up and down the river," he reminisced about learning the back roads of Bucks that included High Rocks.

Climbers making their way up the 200-foot-high cliff at High Rocks.

Michener was a straight-A student at Doylestown High School and earned a full scholarship to Swarthmore College where he discovered his passion for writing. However, he struggled to make a career of it. When World War II came along, he joined the Navy. Out of his experiences came a series of stories for the *Saturday Evening Post* magazine. From them, he sketched together his first great novel, *Tales of the South Pacific* (which years later became the blockbuster musical "South Pacific" on Broadway).

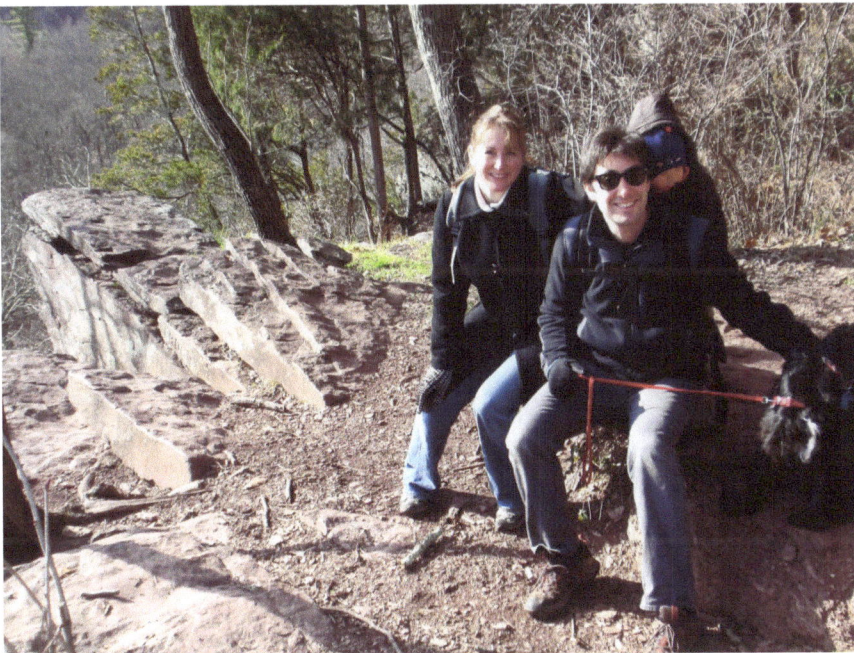
Michael, Genevieve, Dashiell and pet Marcel rest at an overlook.

With the novel's initial success, Michener and his fiancé Vange Nord visited Michener's friend and developer Herman Silverman in Doylestown in 1948. The author had decided to move back to Bucks since land was cheap and it was an easy commute to the city. Busy with his work in New York, Michener asked Vange and Silverman to look for a site to build a home.

"She and I scoured Bucks County, looking for land," recalled Silverman. "She planned to help design the house, and had good ideas about the kind of place she wanted. Jim seemed to have left everything up to her." He added, "As long as I knew him, he didn't seem to care much where he lived, so long as the rooms were large and comfortable, with lots of sunlight."

Carl LaVO pauses on the edge of the gorge.

Vange envisioned a dramatic home similar to Fallingwater, architect Frank Lloyd Wright's iconic home in Mill Run, Pa. "We found a piece of ground Vange liked called "High Rocks" and bought it for about $2,000," noted Silverman. Michener, however, recoiled when the news arrived. "Jim was very upset—he knew the high, rocky piece of land well," continued Silverman. As Michener told him and Vange, "That's where everybody is going to climb up the rocks and kill themselves. You'd better find me another piece of ground."

Vange was very disappointed. But within a few weeks the two closed on a 35-acre property in Pipersville, 10 miles from Doylestown.

Silverman remarked in 1999, "Jim was right about High Rocks. He quickly rid himself of the property by giving it to the Bucks County Parks Department. Even now, with high fences all around to thwart young, would-be mountain climbers, the rescue squad is called out each year to help someone down from the rocks or pick up those who have fallen."

In the end, Michener deeded to all of us a natural wonder. Today it's the place where people like me take in nature with four-footed pals while others dare to risk everything climbing the precipice.

More about James Michener's life in Bucks County can be found in Michener and Me: A Memoir *by Herman Silverman published in 1999 and* Talking With Michener *by Lawrence Grobel, also published in 1999.*

James Michener and his wife at home in Pipersville in a home they built after deciding not to build at High Rocks.

30

HOW COPPERNOSE GOT ITS NAME

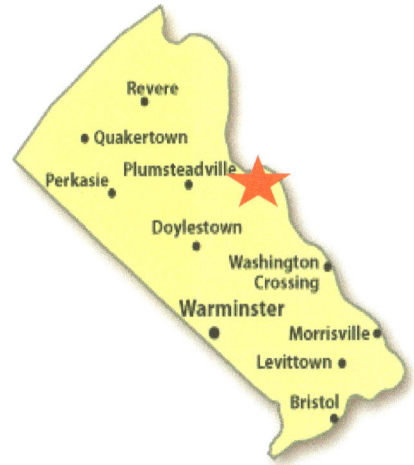

A Tale of Fractured Love

On Lumberville's Coppernose Hill

WILLIAM SATTERTHWAITE DREAMED of romance and living happily ever after. So it was that he got his wish—at least in the beginning.

Bill was an idealistic young schoolteacher and poet in England in the 1700s. Then love walked in. In the midst of a wild storm, he offered overnight shelter to a female student. The torch was lit. "The imprudence of their step dawning upon them next day, they set sail for Philadelphia," according to a letter about the couple written by Samuel Preston in 1826.

Bill proposed and the two married. With stars in

Lenape Indian Chief Nutimus who saved Satterthwaite's life after a snake bite.

their eyes, they envisioned a fairy tale life in America where Bill would resume teaching and writing.

Arriving in Solebury in 1733, the newlyweds moved to the pictur-

Coppernose Hill stretches out over the Black Bass Inn in Lumberville, and the Delaware River.

A snake for which the hill is named bit the teacher as he tried to clear the summit to raise crops.

esque village of Lumberville on the Delaware River. They built a home at the foot of a red sandstone hill overlooking the river. There they settled in and had a baby. That's when things began to fall apart. Mrs. Satterthwaite became ill-tempered. Bill confessed to a friend of being unhappy with his "conjugal relations." Matters devolved into a loveless marriage. To make matters worse, Mrs. Satterthwaite was extravagant in her spending, leaving the couple deep in debt. She tried to end the marriage by attempting to poison her husband.

Bill sought counseling to resolve his marital woes from his Quaker friend, Jeremiah Langhorne, who was chief justice of Pennsylvania's Supreme Court. Jeremiah lived the life of English nobility with servants and slaves who catered to his needs on 7,200 acres in what he called Langhorne Park, which would become the future Langhorne. As a marriage counselor, Jeremiah wasn't so successful; the gulf between the Sattherthwaites continued.

Bill remained faithful while struggling to overcome his poverty. Teaching at schools in Durham, Solebury and Buckingham and writing poetry wasn't the answer. So he carved a road to the top of his mountain. The idea was to clear the summit so he could plant cash crops. That's when a coppernose rattlesnake bit him on the arm. Violently ill, he fell under the care of two villagers who sent for Nutimus, the great Lenape Indian chief and medicine doctor.

Nutimus, living near Haycock Mountain at the time, was the one swindled by William Penn's unscrupulous sons in the famous Walking Purchase. Still, he looked kindly on English settlers. He was a good blacksmith and a renowned tribal doctor. His reputation spread after saving the life of his daughter who was bitten by a rabid dog. Now at the side of the convulsing teacher-poet, Nutimus administered a mix of herbs and roots that slowly restored his patient to health. Others stood by transfixed at the miracle they were seeing.

Nutimus warned Bill to stay off the hill. In the meantime, his wife eloped with another man, leaving her husband distraught. The jilted spouse became disillusioned over his debts and teaching. He made that clear in a poem:

Oh! What stock of patience needs the fool

Who spends his time and breath in teaching school.

Bill lived out his latter days in Langhorne Park. At his patron's death in 1742, the poet wrote an elegy to him. Unfortunately, it did not attract attention nor did any of his other poetry.

Nutimus headed the Turkey clan of the Lenape Indian nation .

However, his brush with a rattlesnake gave the hill its name. Coppernose. People found the heights inspirational over the years. Solebury poet Cyrus Livezey immortalized it in verse:

When I wish to seek retirement, and listlessly repose,
'Tis then I climb my favorite hill, dear, dear Old Coppernose.

How oft I've gazed with fond delight upon the stream that flows
So peacefully around thy base, dear ancient Coppernose.
And there I've seen the setting sun, the day in glory close,
And watched the stars as one by one they lighted Coppernose.

May the summer rains fall lightly, as well as winter snows,
Upon thy crest and wooded sides, old favorite Coppernose.

Bill died in 1752 mired in debt. To settle his estate, his property on Coppernose was sold.

More about Coppernose's history can be found in The Origin of Certain Place Names in the United States *by Henry Gannett published in 1905;* Jeremiah Langhorne *by William J. Bucks published in 1883 in the* Pennsylvania Magazine of History and Biography; *and* Lumberville: 300 Year Heritage *by Willis M. Rivinus published in 2006. Also thanks to Lumberville residents Judy Tinsman DiSalvi and Nicole Case who helped.*

Coppernose Hill rises steeply over this home in Lumberville which hugs River Road.

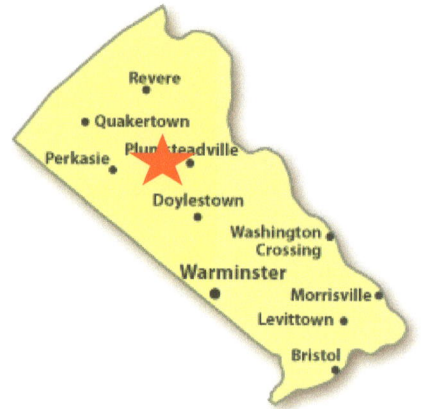

Oscar Hammerstein II Got Inspiration for Broadway Musicals at His Doylestown Farm

MARY ANNE, GENEVIEVE AND I, in the early 1990s, stayed a few days at Fordhook Farm, the historic headquarters of the Burpee Seed Company in Doylestown Township. While there, our host treated us to stories about David Burpee's penchant for entertaining neighbors. One frequent guest was Oscar Hammerstein II. In my mind's eye, I hoped to one day visit the Broadway legend's nearby Highland Farm. That invitation arrived recently from Christine Cole, innkeeper at the three-story farmhouse, and William Hammerstein, Oscar's grandson.

On arrival, I followed Will to a spacious, bedroom on the second floor. It was here, he explained, that his grandfather wrote Broadway plays for 20 years. "Oscar was a big brain and very deliberate. He gave seven hours a day to

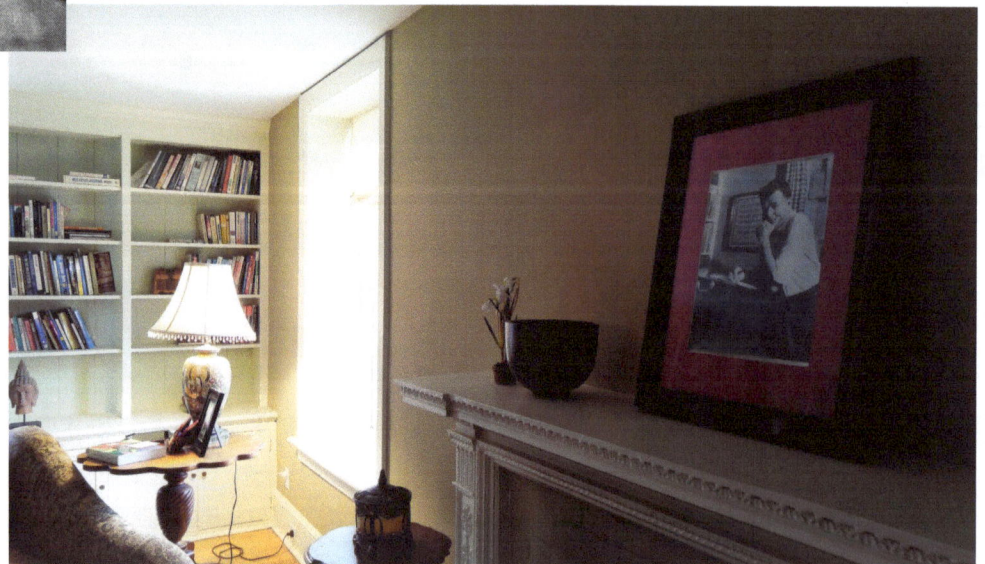

Above left, Oscar Hammerstein in his college years, and below right, Hammerstein's study with a portrait of the playwright on the fireplace mantle.

theater, and one hour to society. After that it was family time when he liked to play board games, swim in the pool or play tennis. When it came to work, the house had to be quiet."

Hammerstein's habit was to pace back and forth in the elongated study, or walk the grounds or into Doylestown Borough, toiling over lyrics to his songs. Pointing to hardwood on the edge of the carpeted room, Will explained, "If you pulled back this carpet, you could very well find a deep groove from all that pacing."

Richard Rodgers and Oscar Hammerstein in publicity photo.

The inspiration for one of Hammerstein's most famous lyrics came through the juxtaposition of views from the corner windows. "There was a cornfield out this window," his grandson said, standing where the playwright's desk once stood. "Out this window was the meadow where the golden haze once shone. A previous owner built a barn to house elephants for the circus. There's even a cement bath in front where baby elephants bathed. Makes you wonder if that's where the lyric 'corn as high as an elephant's eye' came from in 'Oklahoma!' "

Oscar Hammerstein's grandfather was Oscar Hammerstein I who achieved fame as an opera impresario and founded New York's theater district. Oscar II made his own way as a playwright beginning in 1917 writing for the Columbia University Varsity Show, a big deal in that time before beginning

Highland Farm, now a bed & breakfast inn, is where Oscar Hammerstein II worked and passed away.

Stephen Sondheim used to stay at Highland Farm where he learned the secret of writing lyrics from Oscar. The farm is now a bed & breakfast.

his professional career in 1920. His collaboration with composer Richard Rogers was formed at Highland Farm in the early 1940s when Rodgers stopped by on his way home to Connecticut from a trip to Philadelphia. That partnership continued until 1960. The duo produced such mega-hits as "The King and I," "Carousel," "South Pacific," "The Sound of Music" and "Oklahoma!" All of it came about at Highland.

In 1940, Hammerstein bought the farm where he raised 40 head of cattle. There he lived with his Australian wife Dorothy. Their son James, like Will, attended George School in nearby Newtown where he befriended a fellow student who frequently stayed at the farm. At one point he showed Oscar a school play he had written. "He wanted my grandfather to critique it," said Will. "At first he hesitated and asked, 'You mean give you my honest opinion?' 'Yes, sir.' So Oscar read it and then told him, 'In that case, it's the worst thing I've ever read. But I'm not saying it doesn't show talent.' He then gave him a series of challenging writing exercises, which he diligently completed."

The lessons took hold. Stephen Sondheim went on to master musical theater in his mentor's tradition, launching the Broadway hits "West Side Story" and "Into the Woods."

In 1960 as "The Sound of Music" was about to debut on

Hammerstein's Songs That Live On

Oscar Hammerstein is the only "Oscar" to win an Oscar—twice for best song for the movie versions of his plays ("Lady Be Good" in 1941 and "State Fair" in 1945). He was nominated for an Oscar five times. In his lifetime, he wrote the lyrics to 850 songs. Here are a few:

"People Will Say We're in Love" (from "Oklahoma!")

"Some Enchanted Evening" (from "South Pacific")

"Getting to Know You" and "Shall We Dance" (from "The King and I")

"Ol' Man River", "Can't Help Lovin' That Man" and "Make Believe" (from "Showboat")

"If I Loved You" and "June Is Busting Out All Over" (from "Carousel")

"The Last Time I Saw Paris" (from "Lady Be Good")

"It Might As Well Be Spring" (from "State Fair")

Broadway, Hammerstein succumbed to stomach cancer. He was 65. Afterward Dorothy sold Highland Farm. Following a happy marriage of 31 years, she could no longer live there. "It was too sad after Oscar's death," said Will.

It was sometime after Hammerstein passed away that the family physician sent a letter to Dorothy. "At one of his last visits to my office I told Oscar, despite all other recommendation to the contrary, I would suggest that he take a course of X-ray therapy," Dr. Ben Kean wrote. "The next day he came back with these words, 'Ben, I have considered very carefully your recommendation. In this showdown I must really decide whether to die, possibly a little later, in the hospital, or on Dorothy's pillow. I'm really lucky and never knew

Oscar Hammerstein at the height of his fame in the 1950s.

how much until now.'"

Will led me to the master bedroom at Highland Farm. "The last line of the last song my grandfather ever wrote—'Edelweiss' for 'The Sound of Music'—is 'bless my homeland forever.' He wanted to be home at his beloved farm, and this is where he died...on Dorothy's pillow."

William Hammerstein suggests Getting to Know Him: A Biography of Oscar Hammerstein II *by Hugh Ford published in 1995 as the definitive story of his grandfather.*

Grandson William Hammerstein on a tour of Highland Farm's barn which was built to house circus elephants.

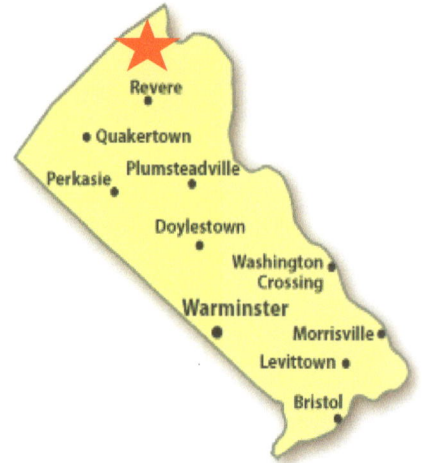

Revere
Quakertown
Plumsteadville
Perkasie
Doylestown
Washington Crossing
Warminster
Morrisville
Levittown
Bristol

My Own Lassie Come Home Story

Dana, neighborhood collie owned by a physician that I befriended when I was in my teens.

I WAS SURPRISED TO LEARN when I arrived in Bucks County that Erik Knight once lived here. No other author had a greater influence on my boyhood.

From 1939 to 1943, he raised collies in Springfield in Upper Bucks. Born in 1897 in England, Knight grew up in rural Yorkshire where dog stories were common. Immigrating with his mother to Philadelphia in 1912 when he was 15, he studied music and art, and later became a respected film critic for the *Philadelphia Public Ledger*. His passion, however, was writing short stories, screenplays and books. One remains a classic. It started as a short story for the *Saturday Evening Post*, later expanded into a novel that became a movie and sequels including a TV series. "Lassie Come Home" was that story.

Erik Knight, the author of *Lassie Come Home,* lived in Upper Bucks County where he bred collies.

My grandmother Ivy, a voracious reader, sent me the book when I was 10. I devoured it. Famous hero dog stories became my staple. I collected and read them all: *Beautiful Joe, Bob Son of Battle, Silver Chief: Dog of the North, Silver Chief to the Rescue, Kazan the Wolf Dog, The Return of Silver Chief, Spike of Swift River, The Call of the Wild* and *Juneau the Sleigh Dog* among others. But the story of Lassie stayed with me. To me collies remain the most beautiful, gentle canines in the dog world. They are incredibly loyal companions as I was to discover.

When I was six, Dad brought home a mixed breed who chewed up the new living room furniture. No more dogs. That didn't deter me since dogs ran free in my childhood. I made pals with any dog in the neighborhood. My best friend Adrian Espinosa had a black-and-white collie. In short order, Cindy and I became insepara-

Author Erik Knight's home on Springhouse Farm where he bred collies in Upper Bucks. One of them inspired "Lassie Come Home" in the 1940s.

ble. I would run across a field, and she would tackle me, all in fun. Going fishing, she would sit right next to me, alert to any tug on the line. A *Sun-Star* newspaper photographer noticed; Cindy and I became a page one portrait. Adrian suggested there be a 50-50 arrangement in terms of Cindy's care: He gets the front half and I get the back.

Dad was climbing the corporate ladder, so moves were inevitable. Our next stop was Harris Acres on the other side of town. A physician lived close by and he had a beautiful mahogany sable collie just like Lassie. Dana often escaped her backyard. The first time I came across her, we became buds. She was my "Lassie Come Home." Whenever the doc wondered what happened to his dog, he knew where to find her. My house.

Collies prefer people to other dogs, and they don't like to be left alone for long. The

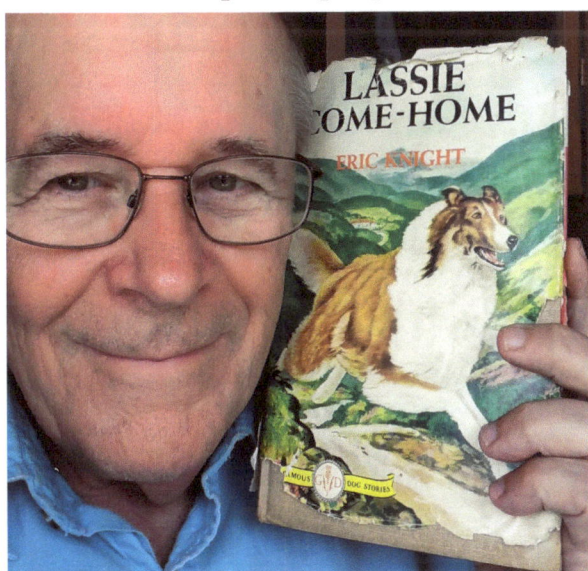

Author LaVO with his cherished book given to him by his grandparents when he was a child.

doc was often busy. So Dana would run away and show up at our place. She often accompanied me to school and sometimes showed up when the school day was over. Together we'd bounce along Bear Creek and the Santa Fe rail line on the way home. This went on for years from junior high through high school. I think doc was OK with that.

When I went off to college and my family moved to Florida, news arrived that Dana had disappeared. The doc went to the home where I used to live. She wasn't there. A month later they found her body in a crawl space under my old school. I suppose she was lingering broken hearted...waiting for me.

Children relax at the New Pond aquatic stream at Bowman's Tower Wildflower Preserve in Washington Crossing Historical Park.

IN SEARCH OF HUMPTY DUMPTY

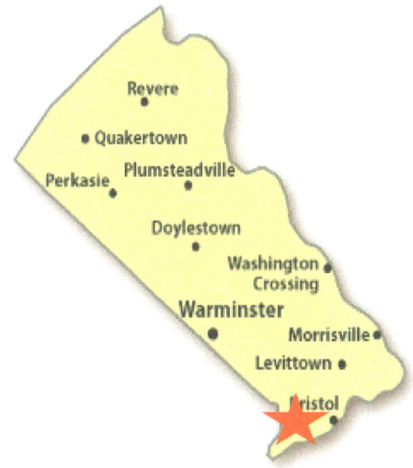

Bensalem Estate Was Home
To 19th Century Art Commune

The author and his grand-
daughter Margaux beneath
Humpty Dumpty at the ruins of
Sarobia in Bensalem.

"LET'S GO FIND HUMPTY DUMPTY!"

With big smiles, my grandchildren Dashiell and Margaux hopped in the car with mom Genevieve and college pal Eileen, and off we went to fabled Sarobia. The drive gave me a chance to explain what I knew about the former Bensalem commune and its nursery rhyme icon.

The 155-acre manse was the fountainhead of Philadelphia naturalists Robert and Sara Logan. Robert, a Harvard-trained Wall Street lawyer, was a direct descendant of William Penn's secretary, James Logan. Sara grew up the privileged daughter of the Welherill family in Rittenhouse Square.

In 1915, the newlyweds began purchasing adjoining farmlands along the Delaware River on the Bensalem side of Neshaminy Creek. They moved into a large manor house on site with a barn con-

Robert and Sara Logan at the time they built Sarobia with its enclosed garden mounted by the stone Humpty Dumpty figure over the gate.

verted for amateur theater. They added an Alice-in-Wonderland sculpture garden behind an adobe wall mounted by a large, stone Humpty Dumpty, his legs dangling over the gate. The Logans idolized Egyptian cat goddess Bastet and made their property a haven for felines. Iron statues of two Egyptian black cats and the word "Sarobia" guarded the State Road entrance to the compound. The name was a contraction of the first three letters of the couple's first names.

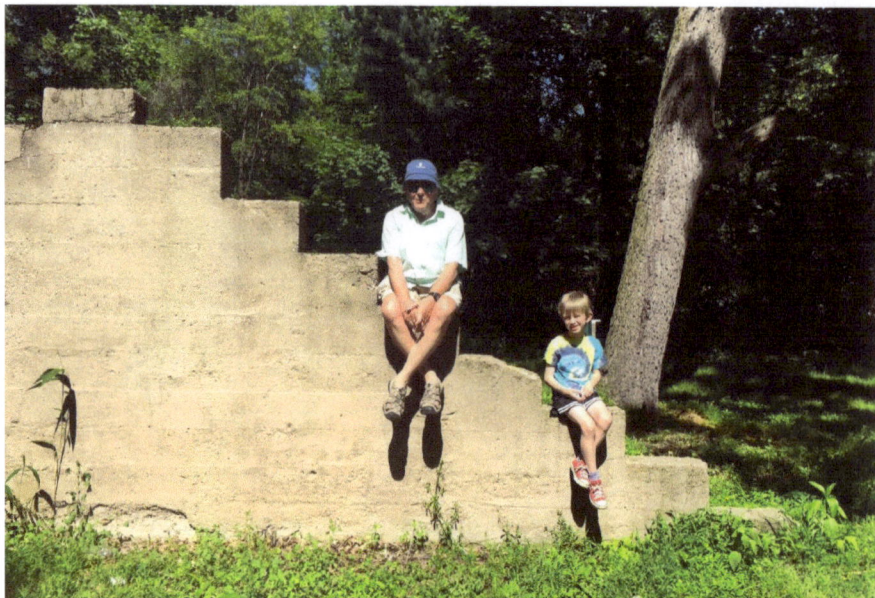

As activists in Eastern religions, the couple attracted affluent theosophists, a movement begun in the U.S. in 1875 that professed reincarnation and Indian religious beliefs. The two took to dressing in white cotton fabrics to symbolize purity and avoided anything made from animals including leather shoes. Preferred dress was Indian saris and sandals.

Among frequent guests in the 1930s were Annie Besant, president of the International Theosophical Society, and Indian philosopher/poet Jiddu Krishnamurti, believed to be the reincarnated "next World Teacher." Besant convinced the Logans to choose a transcendental life by releasing their servants including

Above, the author and grandson Dashiell sitting on the wall fronting the once formal garden at Sarobia. At left, the family gathers around a former sundial on the property.

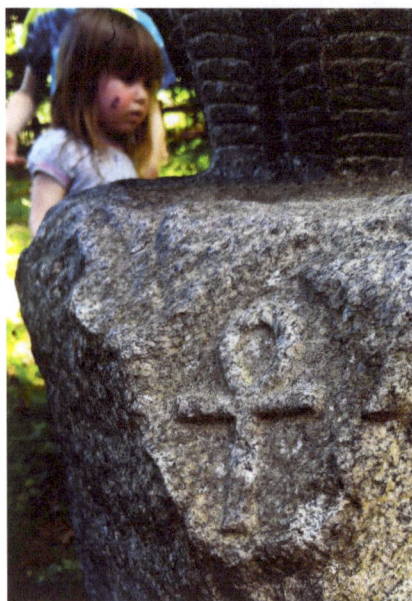

maids, a butler, chauffeur and groundskeeper and turning the estate into an experimental art commune.

Margaux inspects hieroglyphics on a stone pedestal in Sarobia's garden area.

The couple had one child, Deborah, who grew up in Sarobia and the other family estate in Ojai Valley, Calif. After a

Robert Logan

failed marriage, she drew closer to her mom who died prematurely. Devastated, her daughter committed suicide six months later.

The deaths, the black cat statuary and the strange characters living at Sarobia spawned rumors of bizarre rituals, black magic, paganism and cavorting in the nude. Mostly it was guesswork by neighbors who warned kids to stay away.

Robert Logan continued to live on the estate as president of the American Anti-Vivisection Society while writing and editing the *Journal of Zoophily*. With no descendants, he bequeathed Sarobia in 1956 to state government, which turned it into Neshaminy State Park.

Since then, the home and outbuildings have fallen to ruin. Some aspects remain including the garden wall with Humpty Dumpty's likeness. At least that's what we were told with instructions to "follow the trail through the woods." Unfortunately, there are lots of trails.

We took the one along the river and meandered a good hour. We viewed the shimmering Philadelphia skyline on the river's horizon. On Neshaminy Creek, boats slid by. In the deep woods on another trail, a large deer flew across our path. Yet no sighting of Humpty Dumpty.

Dash and Margaux suggested a side trail. Call it childhood intuition. The path soon gave way to an adobe wall. "There's Humpty Dumpty!" said the kids in unison. What followed was "What's that?" and "What's that?" as we passed through the gate to the enclosure. Strange Egyptian hieroglyphs carved in stone, a dry reflection pond, remnants of a wall fountain, pedestals with no statues, a weathered sundial. We had the archival photos of what used to be. Sad.

Sara Logan

Humpty Dumpty hasn't fallen in all the years and is in pretty good shape though his egg is cracking. As for Sarobia, it's just about all fallen down and is unlikely to be put back together again. Robert's hope was it would be preserved "so far as possible as a sanctuary for wildlife, especially birds." In a memoir he discussed living an honorable life, being a ethical lawyer, developing his estate and publishing poetry. In the end, he noted, "I do not believe I have done any serious harm."

A tip of the hat to Kathy Leighton and John Dignam of the Historical Society of Bensalem for their help. More on Sarobia can be found in Traveling through Bensalem 1692-1984 *published by the society, and in Mike Slickster's blog at https://mikeslickster.wordpress.com/2015/04/04/sarobia-the-conclusion-or-is-it/*

The Logans' daughter Deborah who grew up at Sarobia.

Robert Logan inside the Sarobia mansion; he bequeathed the property to the state, which turned it into Neshaminy State Park.

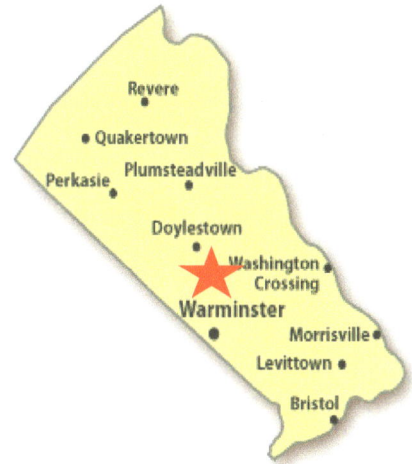

Running of the Pigs, Seances

And When Swearing Was a Crime

There were severe consequences for swearing if you were an indentured servant in William Penn's time.

DIGGING INTO BUCKS COUNTY HISTORY reveals just how different life is today—or not so different.

In the 1880s, pigs on the hoof were a common sight in the farm belt that once was most of Bucks. Those were the days when livestock arrived by train. The village of Wycombe in Buckingham was a key receiving point on the New Hope & Ivyland Railroad. It wasn't unusual for the porkers to be off-loaded and driven through town like cattle. According to one witness, "Occasionally the pigs would get scared at something and stampede, and we would have pigs running loose all over town. The drovers would be out the rest of the day on into the night catching them, often times not finding them at all."

That's when the legend of the great "Running of the Pigs" through Newtown was born. It was Sept. 4, 1882. A railroad stock car overturned near the bridge over Newtown Creek setting loose swine that swarmed the streets. Residents tried to corral the fleet-footed oinkers as they sprinted toward Yardley to hide among the ducks of Lake Afton. Others decided the best

Parkland near Penndel was a gathering site for mystics.

escape route was to float down Newtown Creek. Food for a laugh, so to speak, but the tale was a work of fiction.

Another common activity in Bucks in the late 1800s was mysticism. You could find it in all forms in a village nestled against Neshaminy Creek near Penndel. Back then, the settlement had a Reading Railroad station that attracted out-of-towners wanting to connect with the dead. The First Association of Spiritualists of Philadelphia bought the 114-acre tract in 1880 and named it Parkland.

The village offered one-stop shopping for seances, mesmerism, hypnotism and exhibitions of clairvoyance. Whatever you were seeking could be found there. Knockings, whisperings, table-tipping, suspensions, coals of fire applied to the flesh that did not burn, mysterious ringing of bells and slates appearing out of the mist with chiseled messages—Parkland was the nexus. Spooky.

Bicyclists in Langhorne in the 1800s could be fined for traveling through town at more than 8 mph.

The village is not that kind of place today though the passing of a loaded Conrail freight train can cause things to go bump in the night.

Exaltations over miracles wrought in Parkland were most welcome. But swearing was off-limits. Way back in the day before newsrooms existed, there were severe consequences in Bucks County for uttering an expletive. Take poor Jasper Lun who arrived in 1685 from Sweden as the indentured servant of Derrick Clawson of Bristol Township.

Lun's plan was to complete the term of his indenture, then be free to pursue the American dream of owning a 4-bedroom, 3-bath Colonial. Unfortunately, Clawson was a tough task-master. When he back-anded his servant for not doing his

Running of the pigs was a common occurrence at the railroad offloading site in 19th century Wycombe village.

job properly, Lun "swore several oaths" at Mr. C. He and others heard them. Clawson took the matter to court.

Provincial judges in Falls were appalled. Lun, the court ruled, "shall pay for the three oaths 15 shillings or 15 days imprisonment in the house of correction at hard labour & be fed with bread and water." The fine was equivalent to $85 today. When the defendant's pals anted up the fine, the judges weren't happy. So they adjusted his sentence. Not only would the fine be paid but Lun's servitude to Mr. C would be extended another 15 days. To which Lun swore, "Golly gee willikers"—which no one understood.

Violating the law certainly has changed over the years. Modern forms of transportation led to speed traps. Some of the earliest were in Langhorne. When bicycles became a customary form of travel in 1896, the borough passed a law making it illegal to ride a bicycle on a road through town exceeding 8 miles per hour. (I would have been in big trouble back then.)

You could also be fined for riding on a sidewalk without a bell or whistle, or riding at night without a light. If you failed to ring your bell or sound a whistle at a distance of 50 feet from a street crossing, God help you. Fines ranged from $2 to $25. That would be from $28 to $714 today!

Postscript: Langhorne also ran the county's first auto speed trap in 1912. Cars then could whip by at 20 mph resulting in a ticket. Reminds me of my underpowered VW minibus in the 1970s. I could barely make 50 mph on flat terrain but on a hill, I'd slow to 20. That earned me a ticket for going too slow on the Delaware Turnpike.

More information can be found in Bucks County History: Fact or Fiction? *by Jeffrey L. Marshall published in 1993 and* History of Bucks County Pennsylvania *by W. H. Davis published in 1884.*

Langhorne ran the county's first speed trap; motorists traveling 20 mph would be ticketed.

The Half-Moon
Inn in Newtown
is where artist
Edward Hicks
painted his
famous
"Peaceable

Kingdom" series

REMEMBERING ODETTE

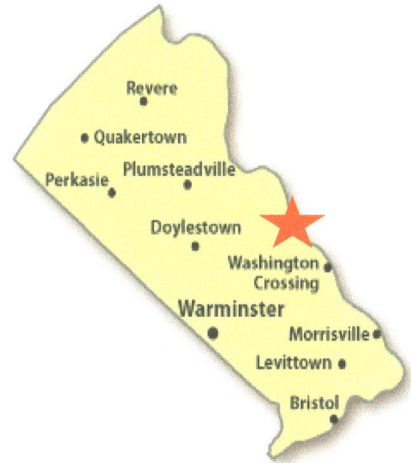

Bucks County's Very Own

Parisian Broadway Star

Odette Myrtil started her career as a musician in Paris. After a career as a movie star through the 1930s and 1940s, Odette opened Odette's cabaret in New Hope at the circa-1784 River House hotel.

IN THE 1970S, MARY ANNE AND I were young newlyweds and New Hope was our clarion call to idle away the evening beside the piano bar at the open air Canal House as mule-drawn barge rides passed on the Delaware Canal below. There was fireside dining at the New Hope Inn on wintry nights. Lunch at Wildflowers. Breakfast at Karla's and Mother's. For special occasions, it was 5-star French cuisine at La Bonne Auberge on the hilltop above New Hope. And accenting all of this was what locals called "the place to be"— Chez Odette. There Odette Myrtil, the Parisian-born star of scores of Broadway plays and Hollywood films, personally worked the kitchen amid the rich aroma of French onion soup and escargot.

Odette Myrtil as she appeared in the 1960s when residents wanted her to run for mayor of New Hope.

As often as possible, she joined customers in her lively cabaret and piano bar where she sang and played her vintage French Boirin violin.

Those memories seem ancient. New Hope today is losing its uniqueness as an artsy country village. The Canal House, the New Hope Inn, Wildflowers, La Bonne Auberge, Chez Odette, the barge rides are only memories. They've been replaced by million-dollar condos, townhouses and corporate businesses. As a former resident told me, "The cool people sold their homes and moved out."

Odette Myrtil symbolized New Hope of the 1950s, 1960s and 1970s. She was so popular citizens in 1965 campaigned to elect her mayor. The state Liquor Control Board put an end to it; no one owning a liquor license could be mayor.

As a child, Odette learned to play the violin, dance and sing. By age 13, she was a professional entertainer in Paris. Three years later, she joined Zeigfeld Follies on Broadway. By 18, she re-crossed the Atlantic for stardom on the London stage and in vaudeville. Hollywood soon came knocking. From 1923 to 1972, she appeared in more than two dozen feature films. Among them "Yankee Doodle Dandy" (1942) and Alfred Hitchcock's "Strangers on a Train (1951). Playing herself, she sang the title song in "The Last Time I Saw Paris" (1954). She also had success as a garment designer for nine motion pictures, and her "Odette" clothing line. On Broadway, she took many roles including "Bloody Mary" in "South Pacific."

Exasperated at how Hollywood tended to portray French women, she once sighed to a reporter, "I have never heard a French woman say 'Oh, la,la' in my entire life."

On a visit to New Hope in 1955, she enjoyed its small shops and cozy eateries where artists gath-

Odette attracted attention in the 1950s by running a lively nightclub attached to the summer stock theater Bucks County Playhouse in New Hope.

This poster on the Delaware Canal trail memorializes the former restaurant, showing Odette serving French movie star Maurice Chevalier at her restaurant.

ered. She took a job for three years managing the Playhouse Inn adjacent to the Bucks County Playhouse and energized the inn's nightclub. In 1960, she bought an old tavern on the lower edge of town. Built in 1784, the River House had been a hotel, general store and tavern for boatmen on the river and the canal. Odette converted the two-story building into a floral-decorated, intimate French restaurant where the locals could schmooze with her and nationally-known entertainers. Chez Odette became a New Hope favorite. Three years before her death and burial, in Solebury, in 1978 at age 80, she sold the restaurant. Today it's falling apart, a victim of Delaware River flooding in 2006. Having survived for 231 years, the restaurant will give way to something far different—a four-story, 34-room luxury boutique hotel. The Riverhouse at Odette's will offer an elevator to a rooftop open-air bar and lounge, a ballroom with floor-to-ceiling retractable glass walls leading to a second-story veranda and an Odette-inspired piano bar and cabaret.

While biking the canal towpath recently, I came across a large sign honoring Odette Myrtil's contribution to New Hope. A photo shows her serving dinner to French movie star Maurice Chevalier at Chez Odette. One hundred feet away stood the ruins of her restaurant, windows shattered and boarded up, gardens overgrown, rain gutters falling down, the gazebo where wedding photos once were taken barely standing and strangled by vines. Sad.

A detailed biography of Odette can be found at http://bit.ly/2aVXA3I and a filmography at http://imdb.to/2bj9kcA. Information on the Riverhouse at Odette's can be found at www.riverhousenewhope.com/

This early concept of what a developer planned to do with the boarded up Chez Odette property

The train station of the New Hope & Ivyland excursion railroad dispenses tickets for journeys through the Bucks countryside in antique cars pulled by a steam locomotive.

THE MYSTERIOUS LENAPE STONE

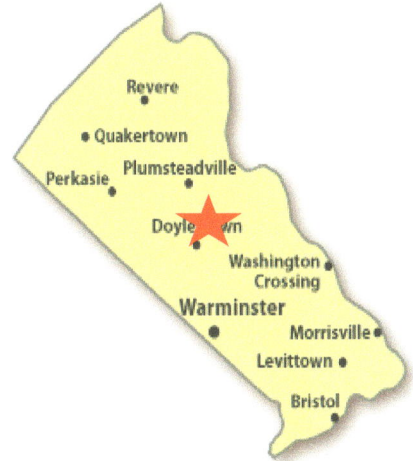

In Search of the Lenape Stone:

An Indiana Jones–Style Adventure

Grandson Dashiell and the author in search of clues to the fabled Lenape Stone at the Mercer Museum in Doylestown.

WHAT I LIKE ABOUT the Mercer Museum is its vast collection of Early American artifacts. Thousands are stuffed into every cranny of the towering monolith in Doylestown. The place is an Indiana Jones holiday. With that in mind, I invited grandson Dashiell, 5, to join me on a recent adventure. "Let's go find the Lenape Stone!" "Sure!" he exclaimed. "I'll bring two

flashlights, Baby PopPop. One for me and one for you."

Wearing my father's Aussie digger hat, I met Dash, his mom Genevieve and younger sister Margaux at the museum entrance. We then wormed our way up seven floors, around and around the museum's cavernous atrium where carriages, row boats, even a stagecoach hung in space. On the sixth floor, we missed a stairway, back-

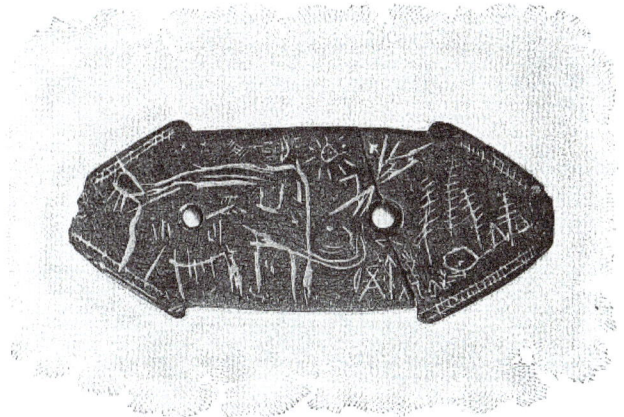

Etchings on the stone appear to show an epic battle between Native Americans and a mastodon.

tracked and entered a darkened corridor leading to a glass case. We trained our flashlights and stared. There on a small pedestal was one of the archeological wonders of all time. At least that was the thinking when the Lenape Stone was discovered in the late 1800s in a farm field in the nearby village of Lahaska in Buckingham Township. The flat slate relic is just 4-1/2 inches long, fractured in two and pointed at each end. Tiny holes on the extremities suggest its use as a pendant.

Bernard Hansel found the larger portion in 1872 while tilling soil. Always on the lookout for Indian relics, he'd collected lots of them—arrowheads, tomahawks, spear points. This was different. The stone had etchings including the

Mercer and his dog Rollo.

Lots to see for Dash and the author (in his father's Digger Hat from Australia) at the Mercer Museum in Doylestown.

outline of an elephant, its tusks lowered. Hansel added the rock to his collection and paid no further attention. Nine years later, he sold everything for $2.50 to neighbor Henry Paxson who wondered if the rest of the special stone could be found. Two months later, Hansel amazingly produced it after a field search. The two pieces fit together perfectly, completing an amazing mosaic—a battle between Indians and a 13-foot-tall hairy mastadon, his leg crushing one of them.

Paxson displayed the stone before the Bucks County Historical Society where Henry Mercer decided to take a closer look. As a young Harvard/Penn-educated archeologist, he believed the "queer stone" was a prehistoric pendant dating back at least 10,000 years. Mercer

The Mercer Museum built by the archeologist in the early 1900s in Doylestown to house his vast collection of Early American implements.

made sense of the etchings: "The monster, angry, and with erect tail, approaches the forest, in which, through the pine trunks, are seen the wigwams of an Indian village. Four human forms confront the monster, the first holds in his right hand a bow from which the arrow just discharged is sticking in the side of the enraged beast...A fourth figure is easily distinguishable trampled under the fore feet of the mammoth."

Mercer published his findings in 1885, making him famous. But he forewarned in "The Lenape Stone – The Indian and the Mammoth" that the etchings could be phony. There were no witnesses to the discovery. The pendant also had been polished, destroying any soil samples to help authenticate it. Skeptics soon weighed in. Photos showed lines of the pictoglyph didn't quite match up between the two sides of the stone, as if they were carved at different times. Conclusion: archaeological forgery. Museum curator Cory Amsler agrees. He told me Mercer had hoped the stone would be proof of a "vanished race" of Indians dating back to the time of mastadons. "He was like Fox Mulder of the 'X-Files'—he wanted to believe," said Amsler. "He couldn't completely separate himself as a scientist."

Is the Lenape Stone a fraud? Today in its glass vestibule, its origin remains unknown.

This stairway to the 5th level of the Mercer Museum leads to the Lenape Stone on display behind a glass enclosure.

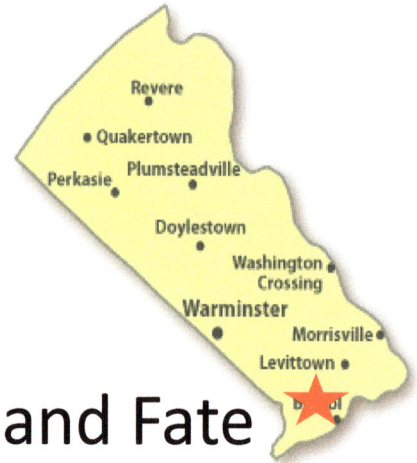

Amazing Grace: Valor, Tenacity and Fate Spared Bucks County Civil War Hero

Statue of Michael Dougherty in Bristol Borough memorializes his incredible valor and survival against all elements in the Civil War.

THE LAST TIME MICHAEL DOUGHERTY dressed in uniform he was in his 80s. For decades, the U.S. Army veteran marched proudly in every holiday parade. Pinned to his chest was a 5-pointed gold star descending from a Stars-and-Stripes ribbon. That medal was the nation's highest military award. The Medal of Honor presented by Congress. Parade-goers knew his story. The whole town knew. What he accomplished and what he survived is incredible.

Michael came to Bucks County in 1859 as a 15-year-old Irish immigrant whose family settled in Bristol. Three years later the Civil War erupted. Just 17, Michael enlisted in the Second Irish Dragoons of the 13th Pennsylvania Cavalry. It was Aug. 8, 1862.

Depiction of the second battle of Winchester where Pvt. Dougherty earned recognition from his commander.

Over the next seven months the tall, blond, blue-eyed horse soldier saw action in Antietam, Cedar Creek, Winchester, Strasburg and Middletown in Virginia. In Shenandoah Valley on Feb. 28, 1863 his horse was shot out from under him. Held for three months in Richmond, Dougherty rejoined his company following a prisoner exchange—just in time to experience his first major conflict.

Union forces were overmatched at the second battle of Winchester on June 13-15 as Confederates marched north to Gettysburg. Michael earned a gold medal for valor from his general as a courier on the battlefield.

By the fall, his company guarded 6,900 Union troops encamped along the Rappahanock River in Jefferson, Va. The enemy attacked at 6 a.m. on Oct. 13. Dougherty led a charge across an open field to drive snipers from a stone barn. There the Irish cavalrymen resisted repeated counterattacks, preventing 25,000 Confederate troops from flanking the Union army in its retreat.

Michael Dougherty later in life as a town councilman in his hometown of Bristol.

By 5 p.m., Dougherty and his regiment were out of ammunition and forced to surrender. They would spend the rest of the war in Georgia's notorious Andersonville Prison. Of 45,000 Union prisoners there, 13,000 died as illustrated in Dougherty's secret diary. "We can see wagons haul away bodies from the deadhouse, like so much dirt, as many as 20 bodies piled into one wagon," he wrote on May 15, 1864. By July conditions worsened. "It is so hot we are almost roasted. There were 127 of my regiment captured the day I was, and of that number 81 have since died, and the rest are more dead than alive."

Dougherty was reduced to a skeleton, sickly and in the stockade's hospital. "The surgeons have had their hands full taking off arms and legs. The groans of the sick and dying are terrible. They cry in their dying agony for a mother, a wife, child or friend to come to them. Oh, Lord of Heaven, it is awful, awful!" He made a final note of "no hope . . . . Guess my time has

Notorious Andersonville Prison in Georgia where Dougherty and his company were prisoners of the Confederacy; he was the only one in his company to survive.

come."

When the war ended in April 1865, Michael was the only survivor of his company. In Vicksburg, Miss., he boarded a steamship with 2,800 liberated Union prisoners. At an overnight stop in Memphis on April 23, a boiler exploded, turning the Sultana into an inferno. More than 1,800 burned to death. Dougherty jumped overboard, taking only his diary. In the illumination of the burning ship, he saw an island, swam for it and staggered ashore. There he awaited rescue.

On June 25, Michael Dougherty stepped from a train in Bristol into the tearful embrace of his mother and three sisters. He had been gone three years. He was only 20. Bristol showered him with accolades. In later life, he worked various jobs and married local girl Rose Magee who bore him 12 children. He served as councilman between 1880 and 1882 and was active in the Ancient Order of Hibernians.

Michael Dougherty's Medal of Honor, the nation's highest award for military valor.

Congress awarded him the Medal of Honor in 1897. In 1908, he published his wartime diary, exposing Andersonville's horrors. Five years later, he addressed a throng at Gettysburg at the 50th anniversary of the decisive battle of the Civil War. He spoke of his dramatic charge to take the barn in Jefferson. Holding the fortification against the Confederate army saved 2,500 Union soldiers, he said. So moved was the crowd, Dougherty said, "My hands were almost shaken off me."

He lived the rest of his life in Bristol and passed away on Feb. 19, 1930 at 85. He was buried in the borough's St. Marks Roman Catholic Churchyard. Today, a statue of him in uniform stands astride Bristol's beauti-

The Sultana explodes and is swept by fire with Dougherty aboard.

ful Delaware Canal lagoon park on Jefferson Avenue. He's peering south, his rifle at the ready as if on guard. It's a permanent reminder of the resolute courage of Private Michael Dougherty when his country most needed him.

My thanks to Bristol's Grundy Library and historians Harold and Carol Mitchener for their help in researching this piece.

BUCKS COUNTY'S HAUNTED MOUNTAIN

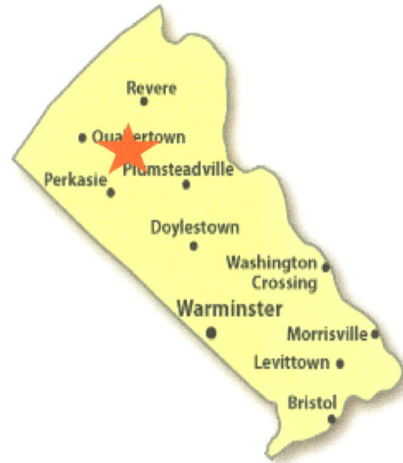

The Mystique

of Haycock Mountain

DOES A GROUP OF ALBINO CANNIBALS hiding in trees really live there? Was this where Lenape Indians had their final showdown with wooly mammoths? Is it true that if you turn your car off and on three times there, it won't start again? And what about stories of subterranean tunnels, Indian burial grounds and an old woman seen knitting through the window of her home but you can see right through her?

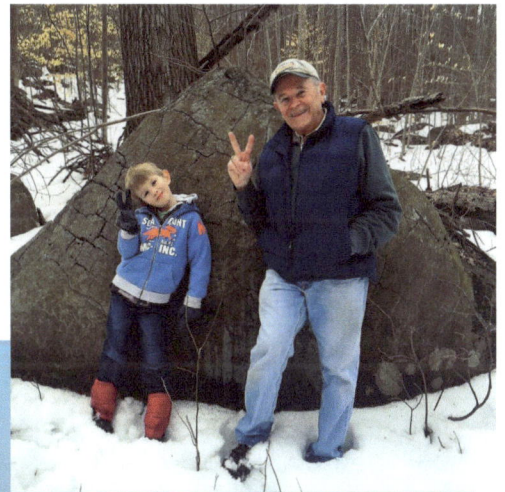

That's some of the lore associated with Ghost

Mysterious Haycock Mountain, which daughter Genevieve, son Dashiell, and the author climbed after a snowstorm, pausing for pictures beneath the strange boulders the mountain is known for.

Well-kept farms ring the mountain's base.

Mountain in Upper Bucks. To the less superstitious, it's Haycock Mountain. At nearly 1,000 feet high, it's the tallest entirely within the county and overlooks the northeastern shore of Lake Nockamixon.

Dashiell, Genevieve and I took a look in March. We're always up for historical adventure. So we rolled out the topographical maps on the table of my daughter's Bedminster home and planned a route to dirt roads close to the peak. Heading out, we trekked up Elephant and Bedminster roads, turned onto Route 611 and jumped off on Mountain View Drive. The name Haycock derives from early settlers who cleared woods for pastures. A jumble of house-sized stones on the mountaintop conjured up a conical-shaped cock of hay, familiar bundled tufts of upright hay during the harvest.

It's no wonder the hill has morphed into a superstition mountain. Nearby are Devil's Hole, Witches Head, Lonely Cottage Road and Gallows Hill Road. One observer surmised, "Good housewives, in olden times, firmly believed that many of the ills that befell the community might, with truth, be attributed to the proximity of Devil's Hole and Witches Head." A visitor once noted, "You can really get a sense of bad vibes around that area."

But this was a bright day. No fear. What we knew is Haycock Mountain is littered with enormous boulders. One at the top is flat, smooth, "as large as a skating rink" and suspended by 20-foot high stone pillars. These wonders that Sisyphus might admire are hard to reach, however. Tangled underbrush can easily get you lost. But if you arrive, what a sight to behold. Early settlers claimed that on a clear day one could see sailing ships on the Delaware off Bristol more than 50 miles away.

Our aim was to find a trail to the summit. We meandered around on Saw Mill, Stoney Garden and Haycock Run roads past fine fieldstone mansions,

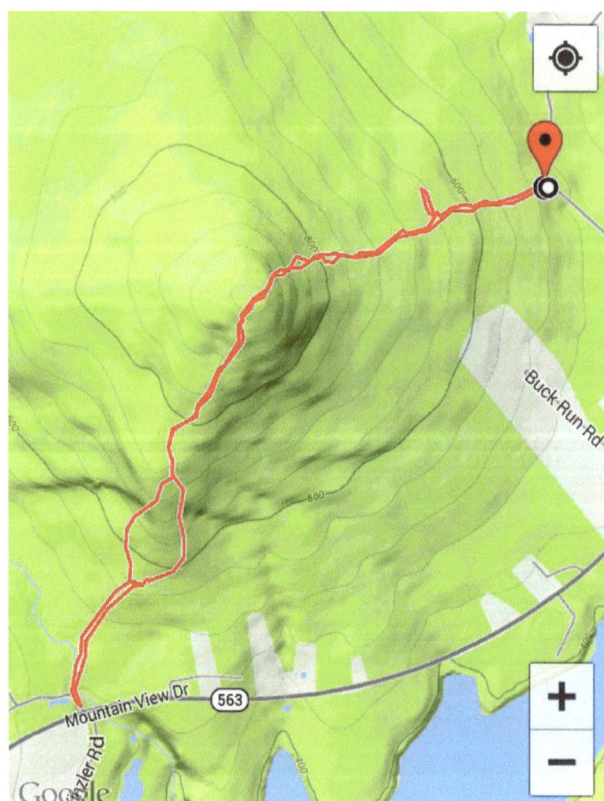

Hiking club map shows trail over the top of Haycock Mountain.

barns with hex signs and broken down farmsteads, one with plywood sheets leading to a spooky house. "Chicken Crossing" was posted outside another. On reaching Top Rock Road, we spied a small parking area and found the trail, buried in snow. We started our climb. As we got higher, the stones got larger. Coming upon a tall pyramid of rock, I mentioned to Dashiell that it was volcanic. "What's that?" he insisted. I simplified: It was formed by hot lava in the days of the dinosaurs.

Near the summit, a jumble of rocks larger than a house.

He knew about hot lava and was afraid it would burn his fingers. I assured him it had cooled off by leaning against the stone.

Genevieve led the way higher to even larger rocks, one of which we climbed. But deepening snow and tangled brambles forced an end to our quest. With the sun getting lower, we headed back, playfully exchanging shouts that echoed down the slope. All was well. No cannibals. No ghostly apparitions. And we proved you could turn the engine of your car off and on three times and it still would fire up on the fourth.

More information about Haycock Mountain can be found in Place Names in Bucks County *by George MacReynolds published in 1942.*

Landowners have made use of the unusual rock formations found on Haycock Mountain.

Route 13 in Bristol Was Designed

300 Years Ago to Link the American Colonies

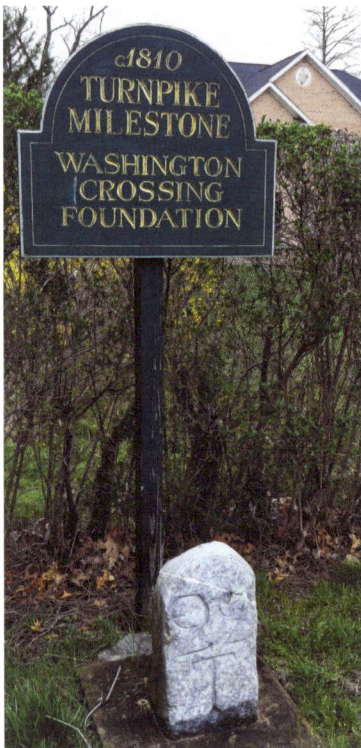

Marble mileposts from when the highway became a toll road are still in evidence on Radcliffe Street.

MANY OF US HAVE STEWED FOR YEARS over the slow pace of reconstruction occurring on U.S. Route 13 in Lower Bucks. Traffic snarls are a way of life as work to modernize the highway crawls along.

Route 13 was once "the King's Highway," the first road built to link all the British Colonies in America and the first public road laid out in Bucks County. It was conceived in 1650 by King Charles II of England and took 85 years to complete. (Don't show PennDOT this column, please.)

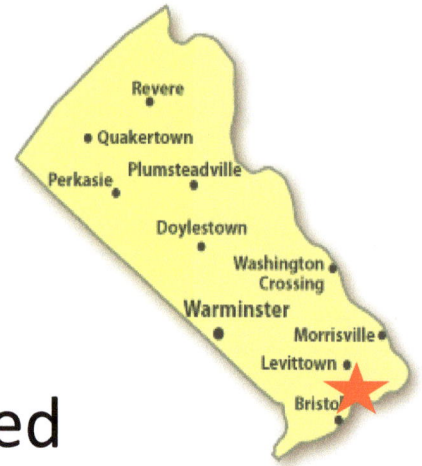

Under the king's plan, the road was designed for horse-drawn carts. It would stretch 1,300 miles from Boston to Charleston, S.C. to speed trade and travel and unify the 13 colonies.

The route originally was "the King's Path"—but a different king. It was a foot trail used by Dutch settlers in the Delaware Valley to exchange Dutch Royal Mail with New Amsterdam (original name for the Big Apple) using paid Indian runners.

King Charlie was determined to minimize Dutch in-

King Charles II

fluence. So he decided to improve the path. Make it a Colonial version of I-95. By the 1700s, the portion running between Morrisville and Philly through Bristol would be a speedway. English Royal Mail stagecoaches would pass at an astounding 25 miles per hour. Steel wheels and hooves of four-horse teams would churn up dust twisters as they hurtled by.

In Lower Bucks, the highway was supposed to follow a more-or-less straight line between Philadelphia's border and Morrisville as decreed by the Pennsylvania Provincial Council on Nov. 19, 1686. In Bristol, it would follow Pond Street, bypassing the business district on Mill and Radcliffe streets.

From its inception, the borough had evolved along the riverfront and its import-export wharf. Four hotels—King of Prussia, Cross Keys, General Brown and today's King George II—had prospered near the wharf. To locals, it'd be nice to have the highway re-routed so stagecoaches and carriages of the 1 percent passed in front of the hotels. Maybe even stop and spend a few quid.

What could make this happen? Money, of course.

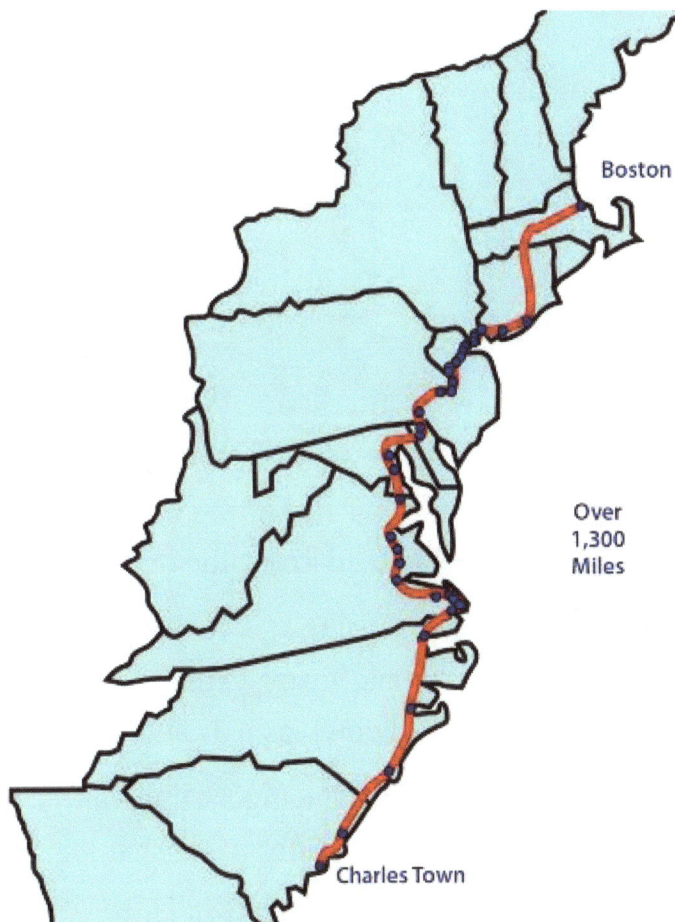

The map shows the route of the King's Highway established in the early history of the American colonies.

The highway was re-routed past the King George II inn on Radcliffe Street in Bristol after the city paid for the change.

The provincial council studied the request. OK, it concluded, but Bristol would have to ante up what amounts to $150,000 in today's currency. Plus be responsible for repairing and maintaining culverts beneath the new highway. Agreed.

In the end, King's Highway coming out of Philadelphia made a hard right on Mill off

The Continental Army used the highway during the American Revolution.

Pond, traveled four blocks to the King George II, then a sharp left on Radcliffe going north to the edge of town where it rejoined Pond and headed for Morrisville.

By the 19th century, highway maintenance strained government budgets. So King's Highway in Bucks was sold in 1803 to investors who turned it into the Frankford and Bristol Turnpike. Tolls were charged, turning a 10 percent profit. Also marble milestones were planted, each with an engraved "T" and a number so travelers could know the distance to Philadelphia's Market Street.

By 1926 the turnpike was reclassified U.S. Route 13 and became a freeway. With the advent of large trucks and faster vehicles, the highway was again re-routed to its present course from Croydon to Tullytown as a 3- and 4-lane highway beside the Amtrak high speed rail line.

Today, the original King's Highway is called Old Bristol Pike. The mileage posts and history books remind us of our past. That legacy is special.

Two years before the American Revolution, John Adams passed through Bristol on the highway to meet Benjamin Rush and Thomas Mifflin to map out what Adams later called the "color, complexion and character to the whole policy of the United States." In 1781, the Continental Army marched through on their way to a decisive

Royal mail coaches used the King's Highway to speed up and down the Eastern Seaboard.

victory at Yorktown. And in 1789, Washington followed the highway through Bristol to his first presidential inauguration in Manhattan. As for King Charlie, he nor any other English monarch,ever traveled the road he inspired.

More information can be found in Bucks County: An Illustrated History *by Terry A. McNealy published in 2001 and* History of Bristol Pennsylvania *by Doron Green published in 1911.*

The beautiful Cuttaloosa Valley is a favorite of Bucks County artists.

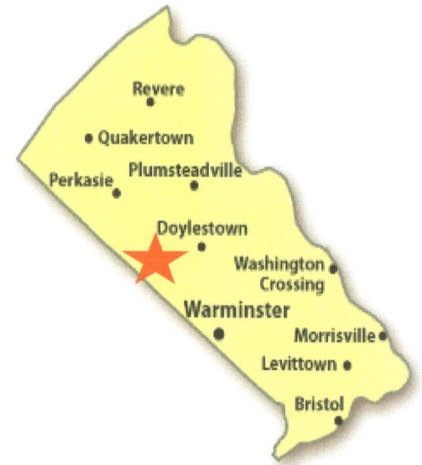

How Franklin Filled the Pews:

Ben's Wartime Advice to a Warwick Minister

BEN FRANKLIN VIEWED JUST ABOUT EVERY SITUATION with homespun savvy that if followed, paid dividends. Such was the case in 1756 when he was an army colonel fighting for the British.

Franklin, a wealthy Philadelphian of international stature due to his discovery of electricity while flying a kite in Bensalem, raised a regiment of 560 soldiers to help the Redcoats. He got himself elected colonel, then marched off to the Penn-sylvania wil-derness to fight French Canadians and their Indian brothers. The frontier at that time was the headwaters of the Lehigh River where a Moravian set-

The minister of this church in Warwick enlisted in a militia unit commanded by young Ben Franklin.

tlement had been attacked with many casualties. Franklin, 50, was to bury the dead, engage the enemy and build forts.

It was customary at the time to attend to the spiritual needs of soldiers. Franklin was fortunate to have with him Rev. Charles Beatty of the Neshaminy Presbyterian Church of Warwick in Central Bucks County. The minister was an ardent patriot and son of Scottish-Irish immigrants.

In the deep winter of 1756, Franklin led his infantry, cavalry and five Conestoga wagons through the Lehigh River gorge heading west. It is not known what skirmishes occurred. However, bitter cold and constant threat of attack was stressful. All the more reason for prayer.

Beatty was a zealous minister who insisted on regular absolution for the soldiers. Yet, at every prayer service, few chose to attend. This greatly distressed the reverend. So he complained to the commander.

Franklin pondered what to do. He knew his men were promised "half a gill a day of rum." In modern terms that would be about half a pint. The rum was distributed twice a day, once in the morning and once in the evening. The colonel noticed the men were very punctual in showing up at the anointed time to receive their rations. To Franklin, the solution seemed simple: Distribute the evening shares at prayer time.

Rev. Charles Beatty served under Col. Franklin in the French and Indian War.

"I said to Mr. Beatty, 'It's perhaps below the dignity of your profession to act as the steward of the rum; but if you were to distribute it out, only after prayers, you would have them all about you.' He liked the thought, undertook the task and with a few hands to measure out the liquor, executed it to satisfaction; and never were prayers more generally and more punctually attended."

Beatty would return home in the spring, then volunteer again. After the war, Franklin promulgated the story about the rum. To the reverend's chagrin, the fiction was born that the only way he could get people to his Warwick sermons was to serve whiskey.

Skipping ahead to the Civil War, it wasn't rum but preserving the Union that brought Bucks soldiers into that fight. At least at first.

In the beginning, it seemed no contest. The North would trounce the South. Everyone was high-fiving and signing up for the army. But after the Battle of Bull Run in Virginia, the Confederacy made it clear the war would be a grueling slugfest with lots of casualties. Suddenly enlistments tapered off. Not just in Bucks but throughout the Northeast. So Uncle Sam instituted a draft. The first sign of resistance was an upsurge of folks becoming Quakers.

Local newspapers also noted "a great rush to obtain exemptions" for medical reasons. Many able-bodied men suddenly displayed physical ailments. Oliver Harper of Falls was found unfit because of a stiff ankle. Henry C. Cooper had gone deaf. William Kelly feigned blindness. "Not right sound in his stomach" got Lewis Moore a waiver. Isaac Chapman of Wrightstown bowed out with "a defective eye." For Dr. Benjamin M. Collins, "white swelling" kept him home. "Unsound condition" did it for Charles Chapman.

For others, excuses failed. Samuel Yate's "weak breast," Elwood Williamson's "weak lungs,", George W. Hartley's "rheumatism etcetera" and Francis Briggs' "imperfect speech" gave them fast tickets into the army.

It would take another century before all you needed was enrollment full-time in college to avoid the Korean and Vietnam Wars. College enrollment spiked during both conflicts.

Sources include Bucks County History: Fact or Fiction *by Jeffrey L. Marshall published in 1993,* Neshaminy Presbyterian Church of Warwick 1726-1886 *by Rev. D.K. Turner published in 1876, and "When Ben Franklin Met the Battlefield" by Brooke C. Stoddard published in Smithsonian Magazine on Oct. 7, 2010.*

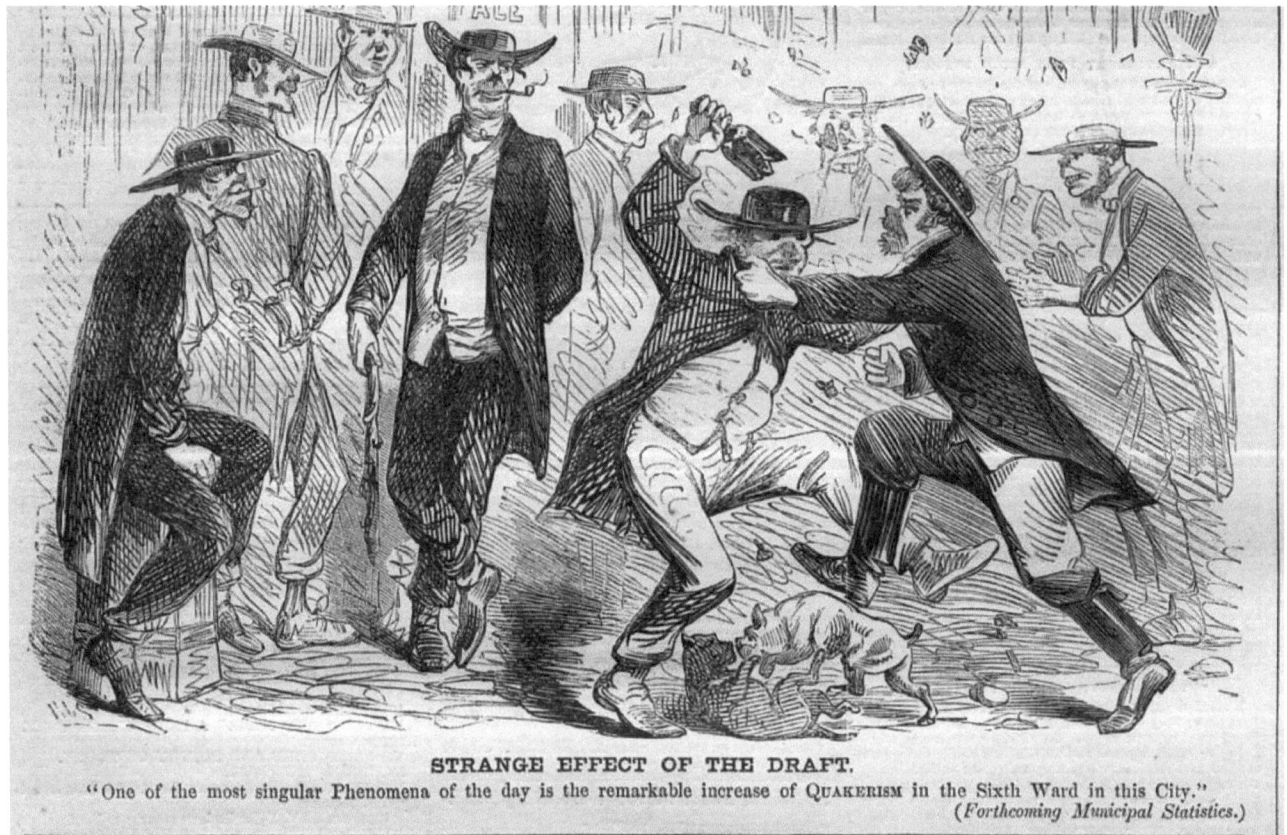

STRANGE EFFECT OF THE DRAFT.

"One of the most singular Phenomena of the day is the remarkable increase of QUAKERISM in the Sixth Ward in this City."

(Forthcoming Municipal Statistics.)

Cartoon published during the Civil War commented on an upsurge in those getting out of the draft by declaring themselves peace-loving Quakers.

AMERICAN CRISIS

Did Man Who Inspired the Revolution Write His Famous Essay in Solebury?

Every kid of a certain age knows George Washington crossed the Delaware River on Christmas 1776 to turn the course of the American Revolution. Yet, before that pivotal event, a two-story farmhouse in Solebury might have had much to do with the general's success. According to historian George MacReynolds, Colonial firebrand Thomas Paine wrote "Common Sense" at the Thompson-Neely House. The 48-page pamphlet was a best-seller when published in Philadelphia in January 1776, a year before the crossing. Paine's call for a declaration of independence convinced many in the 13 colonies that war against King George III was winnable.

Thomas Paine, firebrand of the American Revolution

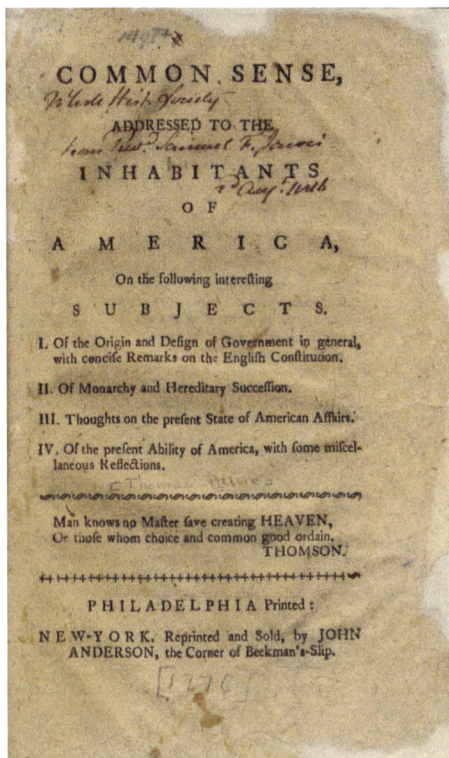

"Common Sense" was an earlier essay that lit the fuse of the Revolution.

MacReynolds' erroneous revelation is in "Place Names in Bucks County Pennsylvania" published by the Bucks County Historical Society in 1940. In a segment on Solebury, he notes, "Tom Paine is said to have written 'Common Sense' at the Thompson-Neely House." Is this true? With no sourcing to lean on, I did a little sleuthing.

The American CRISIS.

NUMBER I.

By the Author of COMMON SENSE.

THESE are the times that try men's fouls: The
summer foldier and the funfhine patriot will, in this
crifis, fhrink from the fervice of his country; but
he that ftands it NOW, deferves the love and thanks of man
and woman. Tyranny, like hell, is not eafily conquered;
yet we have this confolation with us, that the harder the
conflict, the more glorious the triumph. What we obtain
too cheap, we efteem too lightly:—'Tis dearnefs only
that gives every thing its value. Heaven knows how to fet
a proper price upon its goods; and it would be ftrange, indeed, if fo celeftial an article as FREEDOM fhould not be
highly rated. Britain, with an army to enforce her tyranny,
has declared, that fhe has a right (not only to TAX, but) "to
"BIND us in ALL CASES WHATSOEVER," and if being
bound in that manner is not flavery, then is there not fuch a
thing as flavery upon earth. Even the expreffion is impious,
for fo unlimited a power can belong only to GOD.

WHETHER the Independence of the Continent was declared too foon, or delayed too long, I will not now enter
into as an argument; my own fimple opinion is, that had
it been eight months earlier, it would have been much better. We did not make a proper ufe of laft winter, neither
could we, while we were in a dependent ftate. However,
the fault, if it were one, was all our own; we have none
to blame but ourfelves*. But no great deal is loft yet; all
that Howe has been doing for this month paft is rather a
ravage than a conqueft, which the fpirit of the Jerfies a year
ago would have quickly repulfed, and which time and a
little refolution will foon recover.

I have as little fuperftition in me as any man living, but
my.

* "The prefent winter" (meaning the laft) ", is worth an
" age if rightly employed, but if loft, or neglected, the whole
" Continent will partake of the evil; and there is no punifh-
" ment that man does not deferve, be he who, or what, or
" where he will, that may be the means of facrificing a feafon
" fo precious and ufeful."   COMMON SENSE.

"The American Crisis" essay is believed to have
been written in Solebury prior to Washington's

First, I contacted the visitors center at Washington Crossing Historical Park in Upper Makefield. No one there knew of any connection between Paine and the house. I phoned the nearby David Library of the American Revolution. There, librarian Katherine Ludwig pointed me to a few biographies.

Born in England in 1737, Paine was an excise tax collector in London. Angered by low wages, he tried to organize fellow employees. Branded a trouble-maker, he was fired. Despising the monarchy and facing possible arrest, he sailed for Philadelphia in 1774. There he became managing editor of Pennsylvania Magazine. He wrote impassioned articles on political issues including abolition of slavery. What galvanized him in the spring of 1775 was armed conflict in Massachusetts over onerous taxes demanded by the king. Paine viewed a complete break with Britain as the only remedy. With independence, he believed enormous markets for American goods would open in Europe and elsewhere. He also suggested France and Spain would likely aid a Colonial revolt. Paine, 28 at the time, advanced these arguments in "Common Sense". The pamphlet sold out, was reprinted many times and cemented Paine's reputation as "the Father of the Revolution".

A depiction of Washington crossing the Delaware River.

The author preferred writing in Philadelphia's lively taverns and coffee shops. For that reason, biographers surmise "Common Sense" came about in those locales. No mention is made of the Thompson-Neely House.

To further pursue the matter, I visited the farmhouse in the shadow of Bowman Hill on River Road below New Hope. The building dates to 1740 and features a bronze plaque noting Continental Army officers including future President James Monroe stayed there before their fateful crossing of the Delaware. I showed the entry in MacReynold's book to a knowledgeable

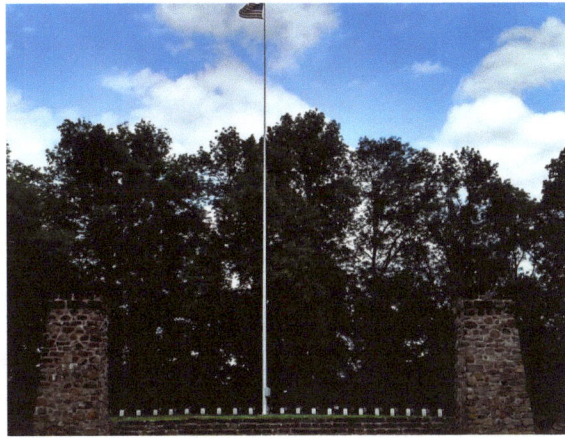

Gravestones of Revolutionary War soldiers buried at Washington Crossing.

guide. "Nope, never heard that. I doubt it could be true," he replied. "Call the Bucks County Historical Society and ask them where they got that information." So I did. Again, a dead end.

I backtracked to the David Library. There Katherine Ludwig tracked down additional sources including a speech by Warren Ely at the opening of Washington Crossing Memorial Park in 1921. He said Paine wrote "American Crisis" at the Thompson-Neely home, an essay published just three days before the Continental Army crossed the Delaware. At the time, the fields around Thompson-Neely, as Ely put it, were the "chief camp of the forces who participated in the Battle of Trenton. Here Tom Paine is said to have written his immortal 'American Crisis' . . . . it was read to the soldiers there."

Ely's version seems probable. With the Revolution going badly and near collapse, it makes sense that Paine would light out from Philadelphia to visit Washington's dispirited troops assembled around Thompson-Neely 40 miles away. Paine captured the perfect essence of what was at stake in the very beginning of "American Crisis". The opening became immortal, inspiring the soldiers who would send shock waves around the world from Trenton:

"These are the times that try men's souls. The summer soldier and the sunshine patriot will, in this crisis, shrink from the service of their country; but he that stands by it now, deserves the love and thanks of man and woman."

More on the life of Thomas Paine can be found in Scott Liell's 46 Pages *and* The Complete Writings of Thomas Paine *in two volumes edited by Philip S. Foner.*

The Thompson-Neely House in Washington Crossing Historical Park's upper section is where the author believes Thomas Paine wrote the inspirational essay "The American Crisis" to encourage George Washington and his army.

Sculpture outside the Tyler State Park Art Center in Northampton Township.

COMPROMISE CHANGED BUCKS' FUTURE

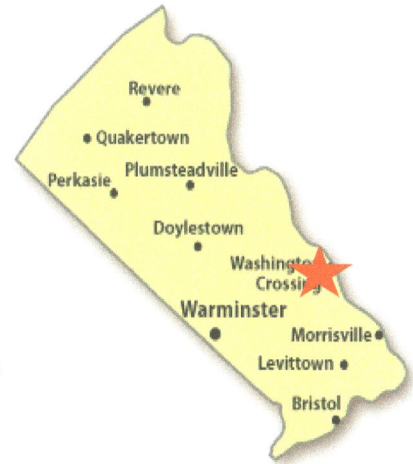

How Morrisville Nearly Became

The Capital of Our Country

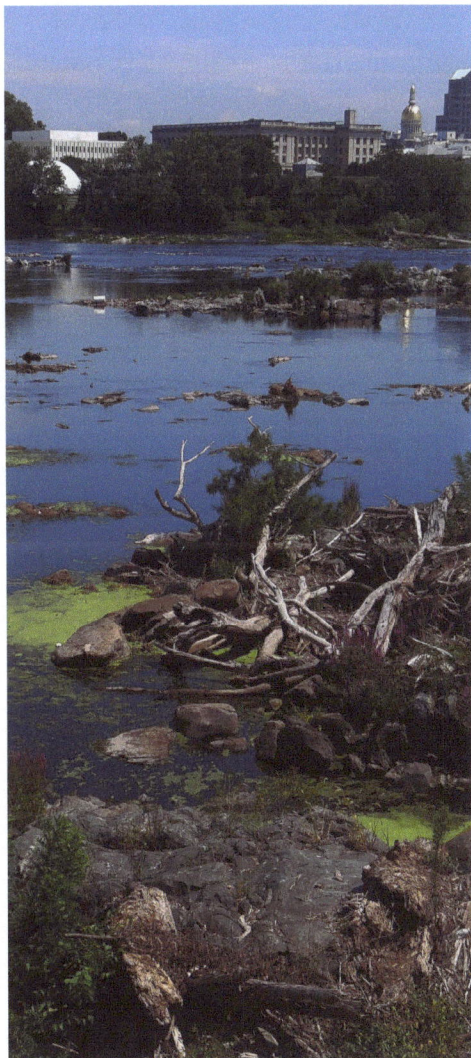

The plan after the Revolution was to build the nation's new capital near the Falls on the Delaware River between Trenton, N.J. and Morrisville.

IF YOU LIVE ON PARK AVENUE in Morrisville, your view of the Delaware River is obstructed by a 30-foot-high, flood-control dike. Climb atop the earthen barrier and below is the famous "Falls of the Delaware" for which Falls Township was named. Across the river stands the golden dome of the New Jersey statehouse, shimmering in the sunlight.

That vista got me to thinking about how Morrisville might have inherited a dome of its own 229 years ago. It would have been magnificent—four times as large as the edifice in Trenton, twice as high and glistening white. It would have been the capitol of the United States. Not only that, 100 square miles of Lower Bucks County would have become the District of Columbia.

It almost happened.

The year was 1783. The Colonies had just won their war for independence from Britain. In October, the Confederation Congress representing all 13 colonies met in Trenton to resolve where to build a "Federal town" for the new republic. Representing Pennsylvania was Robert Morris, a quiet-spoken, immensely wealthy shipping magnate and banker from Philadelphia. Behind the scenes, he campaigned to establish the new capital at the "Falls of the Delaware," preferably on the Pennsylvania side.

Morris was a powerful influence. Immigrating from England, he made a fortune in the export-import business but became disillusioned with British tax policies. He was among those who signed the Declaration of Independence and embraced the American Revolution. He used nearly all of his personal fortune to arm, supply and pay George Washington's Continental Army.

Now, at the convocation in Trenton, Congress decided the new capitol "should be erected on the banks of the Delaware at the 'falls near Trenton', on the New Jersey side, or in Pennsylvania on the opposite."

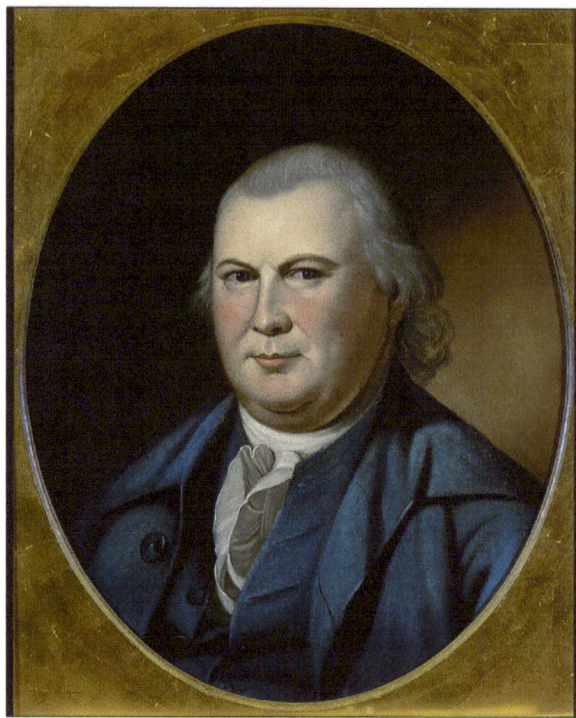

Robert Morris campaigned behind the scenes to make his hometown the site of the U.S. capitol.

The lawmakers appointed three commissioners including Morris to find a suitable site and enter contracts for public buildings "in an elegant manner" for a sum not exceeding $100,000 ($2.2 million by today's standard). The trio focused on the high ground in Pennsylvania, a 2,500-acre tract purchased by Morris. Unfortunately, the government was in serious wartime debt, unable to raise enough cash to carry out the mandate to build a capital.

Nothing was done for several years. Meanwhile Southerners, especially Virginians, demanded the capitol be built near the Mason-Dixon Line in Maryland to preserve political balance between the industrialized North and the agrarian South where slavery was important. George Washington, the nation's first president and a Virginia plantation owner, led the charge, urging Congress to drop the "Falls" plan. With Congress at loggerheads and passions rising that threatened to tear the nation apart, Alexander Hamilton of New York and James Madison of Vir-

Statue of Robert Morris on Bridge Street in Morrisville illustrates the wealthy Philadelphia banker writing a check to support the American Revolution.

ginia brokered a deal at Thomas Jefferson's New York home. Hamilton, representing the North, achieved a complete overhaul of the U.S. financial system to resolve the country's wartime debts. In exchange, Madison got the OK for a Southern capitol as envisioned by Washington. The subsequent 1790 Resident Act approved by Congress gave the president sole authority to decide where to build it. He chose swampland on the Potomac near his home.

Morris would end up bankrupt and in prison due to land speculation in western New York State. A sad epitaph for the man who financed the war including Washington's pivotal crossing of the Delaware in 1776. For him, the dream of a capital city along that river in Bucks County was not to be.

Above top, another view of the statue of Robert Morris. Above, what might have been had Robert Morris succeeded in making Morrisville the nation's capital city.

The Delaware River
at low flow off
Upper Makefield
Township looking
toward New Jersey.

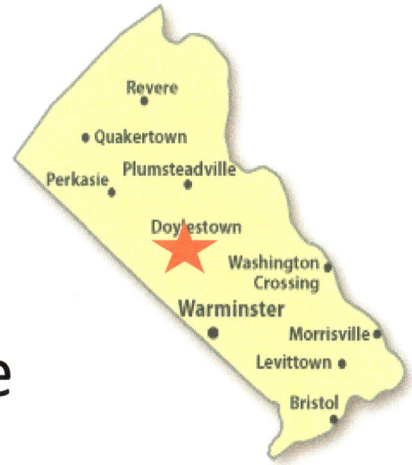

McMansions Now Stand Where
18th Century Castle was Intended

NO MATTER WHERE YOU LIVE, there are people like "Crazy Tom." They weave a life story for people like me to unravel. In the 1700s, Tom tried to build a castle in Doylestown Township, tore it down, then tried to build it again in a quest to turn an old Indian woman into a beautiful maiden. Is there anything left of that castle? Sounded like a cool adventure for Dashiell, Margaux, Genevieve, Aunt Amy and me. So we piled into the car and set a course for where the castle once stood on Almshouse Road. I recounted Tom's story along the way.

Merlin the Magician came to "Crazy Tom" in a dream, instructing him to build a castle.

His father, an immigrant from England, received a land grant in 1727 on the south side of Neshaminy Creek. Growing up, young Tom liked to read stories about English castles, kings and knights. When his father died, Tom decided to build a castle on the family's hilltop where the Neshaminy curls around its base. People began to wonder about "Crazy Tom." They believed he suffered from "too much learning." Dressed in a leather apron, he labored month after month hauling rocks to the top of the hill and chopping down tall hemlocks for planks. Over the years a wall nine feet high encircled open space. But time and exertion took its toll. Poor Tom died in 1768 with his castle incom-

Crazy Tom as a child devoured books about King Arthur and the Knights of the Round Table and wanted to rekindle chivalry in America.

The type of Medieval castle with round walls that Meredith tried to build.

plete. Wrote an acquaintance, "His strength failed, his weary toils were at an end, and the darkened intellect planned and thought no more."

For decades the mystery remained: Why would Tom build a castle? Finally, an old desk went up for sale at an antiques auction. The buyer discovered a secret compartment with a manuscript inside written by Tom. He wasn't mad, he wrote. Rather, he had a noble purpose. "The few and far between people of my race (in Bucks County) are all so occupied in their daily toils that they have neither time nor inclination to think about the heroes of our Mother Land. To them the brave King Arthur and his knights with their table round are myths. Their religion and toil have banished the days of chivalry from their minds."

Tom continued, "I have had a most vivid vision which I set down here. Merlin, the great enchanter of the past, appeared to me seated under a bush covered with white flowers and spoke to me: 'You have seen an old native woman of the country pounding corn upon the rocks while she was drying the fish caught by men of the tribe. She is under an enchantment which causes her to appear old and hideous while really she is a beautiful damsel. If you are willing to undergo the toil to set her free, heed well and I will instruct you what to do. You alone must collect stone and timber and bring them to the top of your hill. You must then build from them

This photograph of a poster, which is located in a pocket park in Doylestown Township, memorializes the castle that "Crazy Tom" tried to build.

a perfectly round castle which must be absolutely straight within and without.' "

If the castle walls were built properly, said the magician, the Indian woman would turn into a maiden speaking English. If not, Tom would have to tear down his castle and start over. With the rampart wall complete, he was hopeful. "I have carried stone and hewn timber and brought them to the top of this hill. I have built my castle only to tear it down, for as yet the woman does not understand me. I will try again if my strength will but hold out, for I feel myself growing weaker."

Tom failed in his mission after years of hard labor, and his timber and rocks were used to build a covered bridge at this site where Genevieve, Dashiell and Margaux stand.

Poor Tom would not last long. With his death, all those stones and planks lying about gave someone an idea: Build a covered bridge across the Neshaminy. It became the longest in Bucks at nearly 500 feet. Yet time marched on and the hemlock span was torn down to make way for a modern replacement.

So what's left today? The five of us took a look around. Tom's hilltop is now covered with McMansions, one striking a castle-like appearance. Down at the Neshaminy we stared at stones that once supported the covered bridge. Returning home, we were thankful reminders of "Crazy Tom" still exist: stones from his castle, a sign memorializing his story and the name for the location, Castle Valley.

More on Castle Valley is in Place Names in Bucks County Pennsylvania *by George MacReynolds published in 1942.*

Tom Meredith cut down so much lumber for his castle before his death that others used it to build the longest covered bridge in Bucks County at the base of the hill where the castle was to stand.

CAPTAIN KIDD'S TREASURE

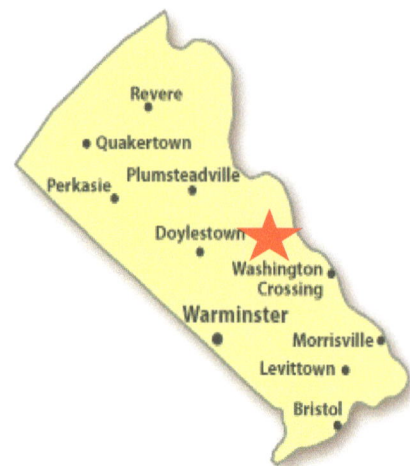

The Legend of Pirate Booty

Buried on Bowman's Hill

WHENEVER MY GRANDSON Dashiell visits, one of the first toys he goes after is a large pirate ship I picked up a few years ago at a yard sale. Dash is adept at scripting an entire battle sequence where captives must walk the plank. Recently, to my delight, I discovered an unusual pirate story rooted to Bucks County. So I asked, "Hey, Dash, want to go on an adventure? Let's go see if we can find Captain

When Capt. Kidd surrendered on piracy charges, he was known to have buried his gold on the coastal U.S. at undisclosed locations.

Kidd's treasure on Bowman's Hill." Who could resist? Soon he, younger sister Margaux and mom Genevieve and I jumped in the car and off we went. That gave me just enough time to tell them what I knew about the hill and the pirate.

Most readers will recognize Bowman Hill as the 310-foot-high mound on

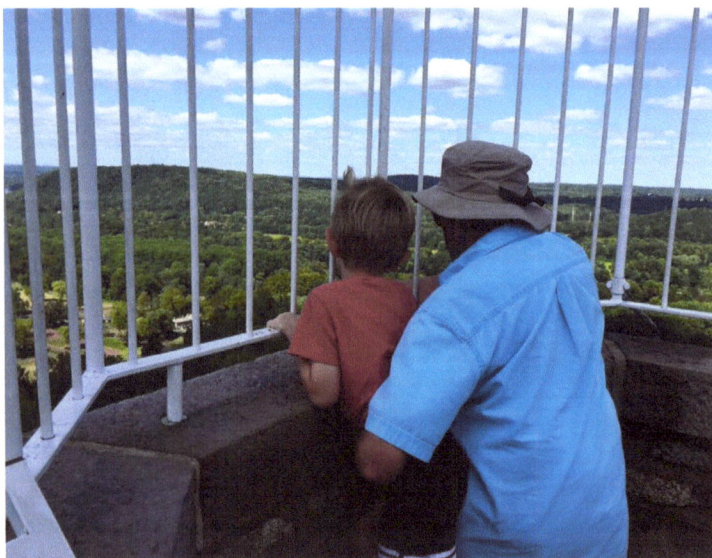

The author explains to his grandson the story of Captain Kidd from the top of Bowman's Tower.

the Delaware River just below New Hope. On the summit is a 125-foot-tall watchtower where visitors can trace the winding course of the river for miles around. The Indians called the hill Wund-achgachunick—"the hill near the water." It was the first mountain Lenape Indians saw while paddling their canoes up the Delaware on return from fur trading posts in what is now Philadelphia.

By the late 1600s, the hill was owned by John Bowman, an Englishman who supposedly was a surgeon on ships commanded by William Kidd, a Scottish sailor who became famous as a seagoing bounty hunter and captain of the 34-cannon *Adventure Galley*. With a crew of 150, Kidd was employed by the British in the late 1600s to hunt down pirates or ships bearing the French flag. His bounty was loot seized from any vessels attacked.

Captain Kidd was moderately successful. But his greatest triumph—the capture of the Armenian ship *Quedagh Merchant* in the Red Sea in 1698—sealed his doom. The vessel was loaded with gold, silver and valuable

Capt. Kidd hanging in chains.

Captain Kidd's body was left hanging over the Thames River in London as a message to would-be pirates.

East Indian merchandise. Unfortunately for Kidd, the *Quedagh* was under the command of an English captain who had secured passes to fly the French flag to ward off local pirates. Kidd decided to keep the Quedagh and its cargo—acts that constituted piracy in British eyes since the ship was not French. But Kidd assumed the vessel was fair game by flying the French flag.

Captain Kidd sailed for home aboard *Quedagh,* which he re-christened *Adventure Prize.* Passing through the Carribean, he learned he was a wanted man, charged with piracy. He subsequently burned his ship, transferred the loot to a sloop and sailed for New York. Confident he could beat the charges, he surrendered in New York after burying his riches at undisclosed places.

Kidd stood trial in London where he was betrayed by former crewmen. Found guilty, he hung from

Capt. Kidd in his glory days as a respected British sea captain who was a ladies' man in New York.

a gallows above the River Thames in 1701.

Back home, the hunt began for Captain Kidd's "200 bars of gold." Supposed locations were islands off New York, Connecticut and Nova Scotia. In Bucks County, locals spawned the idea that Kidd's gold might have moved up the Delaware River for burial on Bowman's Hill owned by his former ship's surgeon. Over intervening years, gold seekers dug up John Bowman's grave on the hill marked by a stone with a large letter "B". Nothing was found.

On our recent visit to the watchtower, I asked about Capt. Kidd. A curator knew the story. But he said there are three stories about the hill. One is that it was named for archers—bow man's hill. Another that it was named for a local settler named Bowman with no connection to Capt. Kidd. And last, it's named for "Nathaniel Bowman" who served under Captain Kidd. He had no knowledge of graves on the

One legend is that some of Capt. Kidd's gold was smuggled up the Delaware River and buried on Bowman's Hill near the future watchtower. Above, the view from the watchtower.

summit. We scrambled around the hilltop and found lots of rock outcroppings but not graves, just the ruins of an outhouse dating back to the 1930s. We took the elevator to the top of the watchtower. The view was "awesome," as Dash put it. Below stretched miles and miles of history and the winding river that Captain Kidd might have traveled. Who can say for sure?

The story of Bowman Mountain and Captain Kidd is detailed in Place Names of Bucks County *by George MacReynolds published by the Bucks County Historical Society in 1942. There are many biographies of Captain Kidd including* The Pirate Hunter: The True Story of Captain Kidd *by Richard Zacks published in 2001.*

ASTRONAUTS TRAINED HERE

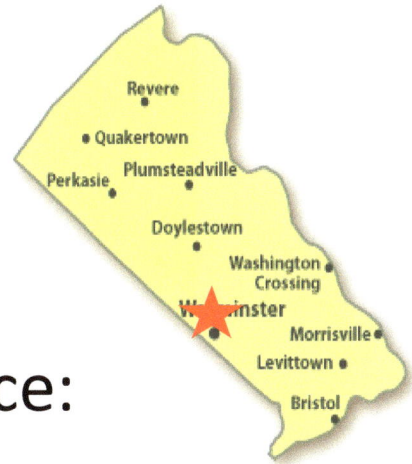

From Inner Space to Outer Space:

Exploring Ties to the Apollo 11 Mission

The centrifuge in Warminster where NASA's Apollo moon-landing astronauts including Neil Armstrong trained.

I'M THINKING OF OLD FRIENDS and a special adventure we shared 47 years ago. It's tied closely to a bit of Bucks County history that helped Neil Armstrong become the first human to walk on the moon.

The author preparing for a deep dive in a Florida spring at the time Armstrong was preparing for his moon mission at Cape Canaveral.

It was at the Johnsville Naval Air Development Center in Warminster in the 1960s where Armstrong and other astronauts trained on the base's massive centrifuge to withstand the tremendous gravitational tug from rocketing into space. Built in the late 1940s, the centrifuge was the largest ever to test human endurance on the tip of its whirling mechanical arm. Navy Corpsman Art Guntner, who trained the astronauts, personally took 350 "flights," hitting 15Gs to set the maximum baseline. That's 15 times the force of gravity. A typical race car driver experiences 4Gs in high-speed turns. For astronauts, it's usually 6.

These days I feel fortunate to have chatted with Mercury 7 astronaut Scott Carpenter at the centrifuge some years ago. Also retired U.S. Navy pilot Larry Zetterberg of Langhorne has become a family friend. He flew the spotter plane that located Armstrong's space capsule on its return to earth from the moon. Larry was amazed when three parachutes from the spacecraft popped open just 1,300 feet from his approaching E-18 aircraft. Larry veered away to prevent air turbulence from interfering with splashdown in the Pacific.

My initial brush with the space program goes back to the mid-1960s as an incoming student at the University of Florida. My roommate's family lived directly across the Intracoastal Waterway from NASA's Vertical Assembly Building at Cape Canaveral. The 365-foot-tall Saturn moon rockets were put together in-

Diving buddy Jim Chupka demonstrates the astronaut-like equipment used to negotiate water-filled underground rivers in Florida to depths of 200 feet.

side. As seen at night from the family's living room window on my visits, beams of light lit up the VAB, one of world's largest structures. It seemed other-worldly against the blackness of the Cape's tropical landscape. To think of what was being planned inside, well, that was chilling and inspiring for both of us.

Skip ahead a few years and my new roomies were two grad students studying physics. One was Max Reed, who would earn his Ph.D. The other was Jim Chupka, an expert in wave dynamics. The three of us became accomplished scuba divers exploring and mapping the state's underground springs to depths exceeding 200 feet. It was very much an astronaut-like experience—and just as dangerous.

On graduation, Max got a job in the Apollo moon-landing program. Jim became support diver for Sealab aquanauts in the Bahamas. Florence Williams, another of our close college friends, was from Sebastian, a tiny hamlet

Diving buddy Dr. Max Reed at the mouth of Little River Spring in North Florida; Max worked on the Apollo mission.

south of the Cape where her father was employed by RCA's oceanic tracking fleet monitoring astronaut missions.

The four of us became a sort of NASA rat pack, often visiting the Cape via Max's connections in the lead up to Armstrong's Apollo 11 moon-landing mission. Max secured VIP passes for the four of us to watch the launch on July 16, 1969. The gleaming white Saturn V seemed incredibly tall on its launch pad

Armstrong and a freeze frame of that first historic step.

even from our safe vantage point. In fact, it was the heaviest, tallest, most powerful rocket ever. At 1:32 p.m., a thunderclap announced the spaceship's liftoff. It rose agonizingly slowly due to its weight. So slowly we thought maybe it wouldn't make it. As the ground shook, you couldn't help joining a chorus of "Go! Go! Go!" as a white-hot tongue of fire nearly as long as the entire spacecraft nudged the rocket off the launch pad and into the cosmos.

Apollo 11 at liftoff.

We hung around the Cape for several days as Armstrong, Buzz Aldrin and Michael Collins sped for the moon. Nearby Cocoa Beach was electric. The whole town was party city. Discos pulsated in anticipation of the landing. Like the rest of the world, we watched on TV on the fifth day after the launch as the landing craft bearing Armstrong and Aldrin settled onto the moon. At 10:56 EDT on July 20 the ghostly image of Armstrong emerged from the lunar lander, climbed down a ladder and jumped lightly to the surface. Chup, Max, Flossie and I walked outside, stared up at the moon and marveled at what had just occurred.

Every year I think of all these precious memories, coming full circle on the anniversary of the night Neil Armstrong took that giant step.

Exhibits and the original astronaut training centrifuge are open to the public at the Johnsville Centrifuge and Science Museum in Warminster. Check www.nadcmuseum.org. To see the author's favorite launch sequence for Apollo 11, go to https://www.youtube.com/watch?v=3mt9znatmyQ

The Most Famous River Fisherman of Them All

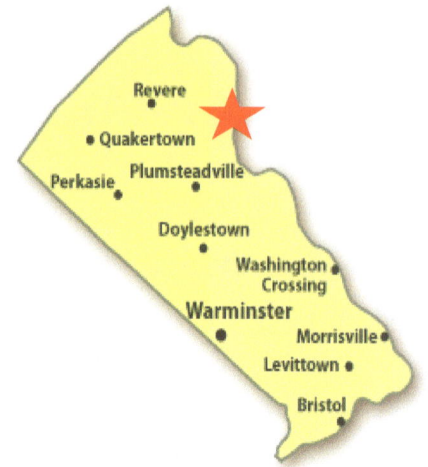

DIALING UP THE WAY BACK MACHINE to research Devil's Half Acre in Solebury, I discovered an interesting account of a famous Delaware River fisherman. Herman Melville perhaps got his idea for *Moby Dick* from the legend of Loof Lirpa.

According to historical records, Loof immigrated to Bucks County from his native Norway in the late 1700s. He preferred a diet rich in fish oil, that of his native land. Most Norwegians live long and prosper on such a diet. Loof naturally was drawn to fishing on the

Delaware, which then was abundant with aquatic life. This was well before pollution from factories in Philadelphia and Camden starved the river estuary of oxygen, preventing migratory fish like salmon, shad and sturgeon from running the gauntlet to spawning grounds in upstate New York. But in those early years, that was not the case. Quite the contrary. Every spring brought tremendous schools of fish. During the run of shad and salmon, the river was so thick with them that old-timers said you could cross over on their backs.

So it was that from March through June of every year, Loof set out his nets in the river channel of Lower Black Eddy just below Point Pleasant. In 1805, he netted 150 in a single night, including the largest ever, an 11-pound beauty. He carted the catch to market in Lambertville, 16 miles downstream. There Loof was familiar, a tall, barrel-chested man known for greeting folks with a big smile and "Morn!" In Norwegian, that means "good morning." His custom was to use the salutation at all hours of the day. Loof was unique for his Norsk ways. He never talked with his hands in his pocket, very rude in Norway. He also tended to be quiet like most Norwegians. It was best not to speak loudly to him.

It was a night in April of 1805 that Loof became a legend. He was at anchor in the eddy when a most remarkable event occurred. He came face to face with a prodigious denizen from the mid-Atlantic. It was a 31-foot-long sturgeon weighing more than 100 pounds. In the gloom, he made out in a flash the large head and mouth and long cylindrical, scaleless body of the gunmetal gray predator. Like a whale, it used its size and speed to gather racing shad, sweeping them into its toothless gullet in an upward thrust from the river bottom. That night, the mighty giant rose vertically near Loof's skiff, soaring in an arc 15-feet above the river, then crashing down in a thunderous water clap that almost knocked Loof overboard. He had never seen anything like it since his days in a Norwegian fjord. The next several nights, he took a harpoon with him. If he could get near enough, he intended to prove his boast about the Black Eddy sea monster.

Every night, Loof waited in anticipation, his spear with its tailing lanyard looped around his forearm. Finally, he got close enough during one of the creature's lunges to land the harpoon in the quarry's side. The wounded beast dived deep, yanking Loof into the swirling water. The monster shook lose. Loof swam for his life. Coming ashore on the Pennsy side, he made for the Black family hotel, dripping wet. There his tale drew gaffaws from those in the tavern. Some whopper, they laughed. With a wink and a nod, they began chanting Loof's name backwards.

a-p-r-i-L f-o-o-L!

This story was published on April 1, 2015 in the Bucks County Courier Times *and* The Intelligencer. *Authored by lra C .OVaL*

Index to Illustrations

Opening Pages: photo of Carl and wife, Mary Anne, from the LaVO family collection, photo of New Hope clock by the author
Back Cover: photo of the author by Genevieve LaVO Cosdon
Page 2: photo by Carl LaVO

The Durham Boats
Page 4: welcome sign photo by the author, reproduction of Washington Crossing the Delaware: stock photo
Page 5: photos by the author
Page 6: grist mill photo by the author, photo of the author by Genevieve LaVO Cosdon
Pages 7 & 8: photo by the author

Discovering My Roots
Page 9: covered bridge photo by the author, photo of Henry Grow Jr. from the LaVO family collection
Page 10: photos by the author
Page 11: business card from LaVO family collection, photo by the author

Falling in Love in Fallsington
Page 12: monument photo by the author, photos of the author from the LaVO family
Page 13 & 14: photos by the author

Amazing Grace at Mt. Gilead
Page 15: photos by the author
Page 16: William Penn drawing: http://americancolonialsettlements-d.blogspot.com/, photo by the author
Page 17: photos by the author

A Castle for Aunt Lela
Page 18: portraits of Elizabeth Chapman Lawrence and Henry Chapman Mercer courtesy of the Bucks County Historical Society
Page 19: photos by the author
Page 20: portraits of Charles Dickens, Queen Victoria and Prince Albert courtesy of the Bucks County Historical Socety, photo of castle by the author

A Haven for Burr
Page 21: portraits of Aaron Burr and Alexander Hamilton: http://www.revolutionary-war-and-beyond.com
Page 22: woodcut of duel: http://theburrhamiltonduel.weebly.com
Page 23: photo by the author

The Ringing Rocks
Page 24: flag of Bucks County courtesy of the Bucks County Government, photo by the author
Page 25: photo by Genevieve LaVO Cosdon, pansy & catfish: stock photos
Page 26: photos of cardinal, rabbit and dogwood: stock photos
Page 27: photo by the author

A Natural Wonder
Page 28: portrait of James Michener courtesy of the Michener Art Museum, Doylestown, PA, photo by the author
Page 29: photos by the author
Page 30: photo of the author by Genevieve LaVO Cosdon, portrait of James Michener: http://explorepahistory.com/displayimage.php?imgId=1-2-1BF4

How Coppernose Got Its Name
Page 31: portrait of Chief Nutimus: http://lenapehoking.tripod.com/lenape.htm
photo by the author
Page 32: photo of coppernose snake: stock photo
Page 33: Lenape Indian clan symbol courtesy of Churchville Nature Center in Bucks County, photo by the author

As High as an Elephant's Eye
Page 34: portrait of Oscar Hammerstein:
http://www.rnh.com/photos.html?img=6339&gallery=58
photo of study by the author
Page 35: portrait of Rodgers and Hammerstein courtesy of The Rogers & Hammerstein Organization, photo of home by the author
Page 36: portrait of Stephen Sondheim:
ttps://eightladieswriting.files.wordpress.com/2014/02/stephen-sondheim.jpg
Page 37: portrait of Hammerstein: public domain photo, photo of William Hammerstein by the author

The Birthplace of Lassie
Page 38: photo by the author, portrait of Eric Knight:
http://www.lassiecomehome.info/id8.html
Pages 39 & 40: photos by the author

In Search of Humpty Dumpty
Page 41: photo by Genevieve Cosdon LaVO, photo of Sarobia courtesy of the Bensalem Historical Society
Page 42: photos by the author
Pages 43 & 44: photos courtesy of the Bensalem Historical Society

The More Things Change
Page 45, 46 & 47: stock photos
Page 48: photo by the author

Remembering Odette
Page 49: photo of Odette:
https://wikimedia.org/wikipedia/en/thumb/a/a8/OdetteMyrtil004.jpg/220px-OdetteMyrtil004.jpg, photo of restaurant: https://www.fodc.org/
Page 50: photo of Odette Myrtil: http://www.listal.com/odette-myrtil, photo of Bucks County Playhouse by the author
Page 51: photo of poster by the author, photo of new plans for Odette's: www.riverhousenewhope.com
Page 52: photo by the author

The Mysterious Lenape Stone
Page 53: photo of the author by Genevieve LaVO Cosdon, photo of Lenape Stone courtesy of Mercer Museum, Doylestown, PA
Page 54: photo of the author by Genevieve LaVO Cosdon, portrait of Henry Mercer: www.mercermuseum.org
Page 55: photos by the author

Bristol Honors a Hero
Page 56: photo by the author, Civil War graphic:
http://www.cornwallhistoricalsociety.org/exhibits/civilwar/battles.html
Page 57: portrait of Dougherty: http://irishamericancivilwar.com/2011/03/28/medal-of-honor-private-michael-dougherty-13th-pennsylvania-cavalry
graphic courtesy of Mercer Museum, Doylestown, PA
Page 58: medal of honor graphic: http://www.mihp.org/wp-content/gallery/andersonville-prison/andersonville-photo-1864-small.jpg
boat graphic: http://mshistorynow.mdah.state.ms.us/images/717.jpg

Bucks County's Haunted Mountain
Page 59: photo of the author by Genevieve LaVO Cosdon, scenic photo by the author
Page 60: photo by the author, graphic: sepahiking.blogspot.com
Page 61: photos by the author

The King's Highway
Page 62: photo by the author, portrait of King Charles: www.historic-uk.com
Page 63: map by Genevieve LaVO Cosdon, photo by the author
Page 64: photo of soldiers:
http://www.history.org/media/downloads/wallpaper/fifeMarch/1024.jpg
Graphic: http://en.academic.ru/pictures/enwiki/65/Anoniem_002.JPG
Page 65: photo by the author

Rum and Prayers
Page 66: photo by the author, portrait of Benjamin Franklin: http://www.scholastic.com/teachers/sites/default/files/promo_images/lesson_plan/portrait_bf.jpg
Page 67: portrait of Charles Beatty: http://www.thisday.pcahistory.org/wp-content/uploads/2013/12/beattyCharles03.jpg
Page 68: cartoon: http://www.sonofthesouth.net/leefoundation/civil-war/1862/august/h1862p560_Picture3.jpg

Common Sense
Page 69: portrait of Thomas Paine:
https://images.jacobinmag.com/2015/03/34thomas_paine.jpg
copy of "Common Sense" courtesy of David Library of the American Revolution, Washington Crossing, PA
Page 70: copy of "The American Crisis" courtesy of David Library of the American Revolution, Washington Crossing, PA
photo: https://phillyfunguide.com/uploads/files/9229570567493889870-washington-crossing-delaware-dsc-1313.full.jpg
Pages 71 & 72: photos by the author

Compromise Changed Bucks' Future
Page 73: photo by the author
Page 74: photo by the author, portrait of Robert Morris:
http://explorepahistory.com/kora/files/1/2/1-2-996-25-ExplorePAHistory-a0h9u7-a_349.jpg
Page 75: photo of statue by the author, photo of capitol building: stock
Page 76: photos by the author

"Crazy Tom" Builds a Castle
Page 77: graphic of Merlin: https://en.wikipedia.org/wiki/Merlin#/media/File:Arthur-Pyle_The_Enchanter_Merlin.JPG
graphic of Round Table:
https://commons.wikimedia.org/wiki/File:King_Arthur_and_the_Knights_of_the_Round_Table.jpg
Pages 78 & 79: photos by the author

Captain Kidd's Treasure
Page 80: graphic: http://www.thepiratesrealm.com/pirates-images/Captain-Kidd-buries-Bible.jpg
photo by Genevieve LaVO Cosdon
Page 81: graphic:
http://i.telegraph.co.uk/multimedia/archive/03295/Captain_Kidd_in_ch_3295057c.jpg
portrait of Captain Kidd:
http://cdn.historyextra.com/sites/default/files/imagecache/800px_530px/gallery/kidd8.jpg
Page 82: photos by the author

Astronauts Trained Here

Page 83: photo: http://www.flitetime.net/nadc_centrifuge.jpg
photo of the author from LaVO family collection
Page 84: photos by Carl LaVO
Page 85: photo of Neil Armstrong: http://www.anatoliamed.com/wp-content/uploads/2015/02/neil-armstrong-apollo-11.jpg
photo of Apollo 11 liftoff:
https://upload.wikimedia.org/wikipedia/commons/thumb/7/7d/Apollo_11_Launch2.jpg/819px-Apollo_11_Launch2.jpg

Just for Fun

Page 86: graphic:
https://upload.wikimedia.org/wikipedia/commons/6/6f/Acipenser_sturio_1879.jpg
Page 87: photo by the author

Acknowledgements

Publication of this book reminds me of just how many people contributed in a variety of significant ways. It's really quite humbling. As a weekly history columnist for Calkins Media's two daily and Sunday newspapers in Bucks County, it was never my intention initially to produce a book. But there were many, many readers urging me to do so. They were the genesis for *Bucks County Adventures*. To them, I hope this is fulfilling.

Appreciation goes to my family, key to making all of this possible.

Topping the list is daughter Genevieve LaVO Cosdon. Her boundless enthusiasm combined with imagination and inquisitiveness make her extraordinary in my mind. My grandchildren, Dashiell and Margaux, are much like her. Her dear husband Michael occasionally joins us in our romps through Bucks County. Also among my history sleuths are Eileen Diaz, one of Genevieve's college pals, and Michael's sister Amy who hop aboard for a new adventure.

Genevieve, a professional internet designer who works with many authors, set the tone with her design of the book cover. Likewise, editor/publisher Karen Hodges Miller of Open Door Publications carried out that vision while adding splashes of her own to make an effective presentation.

A note of appreciation to my wife, Mary Anne Ferber LaVO, a former freelance photographer and writer. Among our greatest joys together have been canoeing on the county's waterways, hiking its many trails, bicycling along rural roads and visiting historical sites. She's had a life-long love of the county and suggested the stories to include in *Bucks County Adventures*.

Much thanks to my good friend Rachel Riley who wrote the foreword to the book. An honored journalist, she's an advocate of the county's illustrious history through her work as editor/content manager for Visit Bucks County.

I also am indebted to the archivists you have helped at the many historical societies that preserve and perpetuate interest in Bucks County's storied history. Among them are Harold and Carol Mitchener at the Grundy Library in Bristol, Katherine Ludwig of the David Library of the American Revolution in Washington Crossing, Rebecca Hone of the Wrightstown Village Library, Sara Good of the Bucks County Historical Society's Spruance Library in Doylestown, Kathy Leighton and John Dignam of the Historical Society of Bensalem, curator Cory Amsler of the Mercer Museum in Doylestown, Susan Taylor of the Friends of the Delaware Canal, Larry Langhans and Jack Fulton of the Langhorne Historical Society, Fletcher Walls and Stuart Abramson of the Doylestown Historical Society, the Historic Carversville Society, the Solebury Township Historical

Society, Dan Callahan and Boronwyn Jones of the Newtown Historical Society, staff at Historic Fallsington, Inc., Honey Hollow staff of the Bucks County Audubon Association, the Harold F. Pitcairn Wings of Freedom Aviation Museum in Horsham, staff of the Johnsville Centrifuge and Science Museum in Warminster.

Finally, I am thankful to Calkins Media, former executive editor Patricia Walker, current executive editor Shane Fitzgerald and Lifestyles editor Tom Haines, illustrator Tom Raski and the staff of the *Bucks County Courier Times* and *The Intelligencer* for positive feedback and for giving me space to write about our beloved Bucks County every week. May the trail lead ever onward.

www.ingramcontent.com/pod-product-compliance
Lightning Source LLC
Chambersburg PA
CBHW042000100426
42813CB00019B/2945